D1531516

NATHANIEL
HAWTHORNE

Captain of the Imagination

Other Books by Seon Manley

James Joyce: TWO DECADES OF CRITICISM
Rudyard Kipling: CREATIVE ADVENTURER
Adventures in Making:
  THE ROMANCE OF CRAFTS AROUND THE WORLD
Teenage Treasury for Girls
Teenage Treasury of Good Humor
My Heart's in the Heather

Books by Seon Manley and Gogo Lewis

The Oceans: A TREASURY OF THE SEA WORLD
Teenage Treasury of Science
Teenage Treasury of the Arts
Teenage Treasury of Imagination and Discovery
Merriment: A TREASURY FOR YOUNG READERS
Magic: A TREASURY FOR YOUNG READERS
Suspense: A TREASURY FOR YOUNG ADULTS
High Adventure: A TREASURY FOR YOUNG ADULTS

Books by Robert and Seon Manley

The Age of the Manager:
  A TREASURY OF OUR TIMES
Beaches: THEIR LIVES, LEGENDS, AND LORE

Portrait of Nathaniel Hawthorne by Charles Osgood.

Photograph courtesy of the Essex Institute, Salem, Massachusetts

Nathaniel Hawthorne

Captain of the Imagination

BY

SEON MANLEY

AUTHOR OF *Rudyard Kipling*, ETC.

NEW YORK

THE VANGUARD PRESS, INC.

58764

Copyright, ©, *1968, by Seon Manley*

Published simultaneously in Canada by the
Copp Clark Publishing Company, Ltd.

All rights reserved. No part of this publication may
be reproduced or transmitted in any form or by any means,
electronic or mechanical, including photocopy, recording,
or any information or retrieval system, or otherwise, without
permission in writing from the publisher.

Library of Congress Catalogue Card Number: 69–10907

Manufactured in the United States of America by
H. Wolff Book Manufacturing Company, New York, N.Y.

BELMONT COLLEGE LIBRARY

Juv.
PS
1881
M27

AAF-0718

THIS BOOK IS FOR
EVELYN SHRIFTE AND JAMES HENLE
WHO, AS THE RAREST OF PUBLISHERS AND FRIENDS,
HAVE STEERED THE IMAGINATION
OF SO MANY WRITERS
TO NEW CHANNELS

❧ *Contents* ❧

1. Son of Salem 15
2. The Time of Witches 23
3. Five- and Ten-Dollar Schools 30
4. Amid the Pines of Maine 40
5. *The Spectator* 45
6. College Days 52
7. The Room Under the Eaves 67
8. Those Peabody Girls 79
9. Brook Farm 92
10. The Magic of the Old Manse 106
11. The Custom House 120
12. *The Scarlet Letter* 130
13. A Citizen of Somewhere Else 136
14. The House of the Seven Gables 143
15. Lenox 153
16. The Wayside 157
17. Liverpool 164
18. The Literary Pilgrim 173
19. France and Italy 182
20. The Marble Faun 195
21. Sea Turn 201
22. The Mouth of the War 211
23. A Cruel Journey 223
24. The Unfinished Window 228

Appendix 237
Important Dates in the Life of Nathaniel Hawthorne 239
Selected Books by and About Nathaniel Hawthorne 245
Acknowledgments 255

❧ *Illustrations* ❧

Portrait of Nathaniel Hawthorne by Charles Osgood. FRON-
TISPIECE

The old Boston-to-Providence coach.

A stable like the one Hawthorne frequented as a young boy.

Contemporary cuts of scenes Hawthorne loved.

A typical store of Hawthorne's time.

A nineteenth-century "five-dollar" school.

Portrait etching of Sophia Peabody Hawthorne.

Hawthorne's portrait, painted for his friend Franklin Pierce
in 1852.

Some famous Salem landmarks you may still see today.

Hawthorne's office in the Custom House.

The Salem Custom House where Hawthorne served as Surveyor.

Looking out of the door of the Custom House toward Derby
Wharf.

The House of the Seven Gables today.

Concord in 1840.

Historical Old North Bridge, Concord, Massachusetts.

The "Sage of Concord," Ralph Waldo Emerson.

Louisa May Alcott, author of *Little Women*.

Herman Melville, one of Hawthorne's earliest admirers.

Henry David Thoreau, in his traveling costume.

The Old Manse.

The Wayside, in Concord, Hawthorne's last home.

Hawthorne's grave in Sleepy Hollow Cemetery, Concord,
Massachusetts.

NATHANIEL HAWTHORNE

Captain of the Imagination

Son of Salem

 I

The boy Nathaniel haunted the waterfront seeking out the long tentacles that were the wharves jutting into the harbor at Salem, Massachusetts. Often he could hardly contain his excitement as he ran down Derby Street, his eyes always searching the water to see the schooner that would soon dock. He never knew quite what he was waiting for, but the ships, coming as they did from the faraway East Indies or from the Caribbean or from Canton in China, would always bring stories along with tea and coffee, silks and spices, lemons and feathers, raisins and oil, sugar and molasses.

When he was older, Nathaniel Hawthorne used to pore over those old entries at the Custom House listing the names and cargo of the ships that had entered Salem Harbor: the schooners *Betsy* and *Active*, the great ship *Astria*, the brigs *The Three Brothers, The West Indies, The William and Henry*. Whenever he thought about the West Indies, Nathaniel must have been hit with a sudden feeling of anguish. It was near the West Indies that his father, Captain Nathaniel Hathorne,* had died of yellow fever in Surinam, South America; he would never again be bringing sugar and coffee, cocoa and molasses from those exotic islands of the Caribbean—from St. Lucia, from Martinique, from Barbados.

"Sugar and molasses were good enough," the old Salem people used to say, "but you should have known when Salem was a pepper town. Oh, we went mad then." That was when Captain Jonathan Carnes found wild pepper on the coast of Sumatra. He sailed through a vicious coral reef, almost scratching the edges of his sloop, until he made the port of Analaboo. The pepper sold for a profit of 700 per cent, and Salem became the pepper capital of the Western Hemisphere. Those were the glorious days, the old salts used to tell Nathaniel as he haunted the Salem wharf. "That was before you were born. By the time you were born—when was it, boy, 1804?—by the time you were born there were already charts for all of the Malay Peninsula, with strange names like Tally-Pow, Mingin Muckie, and Susu, and those harbors were as familiar to Salem shipmasters as their own bays and harbors."

Nathaniel Hawthorne sat on Derby wharf watching the tide come at half-flood. Soon a ship would dock. It didn't matter what ship it was; he just loved to see it come in. Earlier in the day he had heard that one of the finest of all ships, an East Indiaman, would be docking at the wharf. The other

---

* The family name originally was spelled Hathorne. Nathaniel Hawthorne added the "w" after he got out of college, and it is used in that form throughout this book, except when members of his family retained the earlier spelling.

ships, the coastal sloops, didn't cause such a stir. But the great East Indiamen always did. You could earn a dollar if you were the first to sight the ship up at Juniper Point.

Nathaniel never won such a dollar. Since the death of his father, he often felt he was stealing this time away from home, because his mother had clung to the house as a drowning sailor clings to the mast of his ship. She was almost a recluse to the people of Salem. She did not come out in the streets except at night, and, although Nathaniel could not understand why she did not share with him all the glorious excitement of this world of the wharf, he knew, too, the curious need of solitude she seemed to have.

He often felt that need too. Then, he would abandon the wharf and make his way down the streets, looking in all the magnificent old shops, at the wooden houses, the ships' chandlers' lofts, and stores that sold sextants and all kinds of instruments for those who went to sea. But mostly it was to the wharf that he was drawn.

How could anyone resist the sounds of a ship mooring at the wharf? There were the chanteys sung by the crowd waiting on the docks with such refrains as:

"A Yankee ship and a Yankee crew,
   Yally-i-ho-ye know!
Over the main like a sea-gull flew;
   Sing-hey and aloft ye go!"

There were the shouts of the captain and crew as they tried to bring the ship into wind until, with topsail checking her speed, the ship could be moored at the end of the pier.

"Hard down." The Captains would shout. "Take in the main topsail. Watch out, look aloft, watch that sail against the mast. Step lively, lads."

Nathaniel never tired of watching the ritual of mooring the ships. Every Salem child, they said in those days, had been reared on tar, given bags of sea salt as a treat instead of sugar. The wharves and shipyards were favorite playgrounds. By their early teens many boys would be shipping out; they would see Africa long before they saw New York and, like Hawthorne's father, many would die young of some strange fever in some foreign place. If a man did not die at sea, he might instead follow the sea with such success that his family might stamp its name on a street or a town, as Captain Elias Derby had done in the very street and wharf the Salem boys haunted.

Nathaniel Hawthorne was neither to die at sea nor to become rich—but he did explore the strange coast of the American imagination with more skill than the most skillful mariner, and his name was eventually to be stamped on the history of American literature far more deeply than that of any Salem merchant-mariner in the records of the Custom House.

Nathaniel Hawthorne was born on July 4, 1804. His father died when Nathaniel was four years old, leaving his mother a young widow with three children: Elizabeth, two years older than Nathaniel, and Maria Louisa, an infant. The young family lived at 27 Union Street in the house that has been moved and now sits behind the garden of the House of the Seven Gables. There was little money, however, and the Hawthornes moved to Mrs. Hawthorne's father's home, the Manning House, a three-storied gray house ugly in comparison with many of Salem's famous homes.

Beyond garden walls there were magnificent houses, some of the finest in all of New England. The people of Salem were always talking with pride of Salem's great past. True, Salem had a present, but it was the glorious past, when the name of Salem was known throughout all the world, that inspired the inhabitants. No one quite knows what makes a writer, but many in Salem wrote with excitement and pleasure in their old diaries and journals of the days they had spent at sea. They kept day books similar to those Hawthorne kept in later years, but his extensive notebooks contained seeds of stories and essays that he would embellish and embroider to create some of his famous tales.

When Hawthorne was born, every Salem boy was expected to go to sea. Certainly, his livelihood would have something to do with the sea. Nathaniel's great-uncles on the Hathorne side had all been famous in the seafaring world either as shippers or sailors. His father went to sea as today's men go to work in an office or factory. There was almost no alternative. Salem had great sons. It was the home of Nathaniel Bowditch, who had been the first to study navigation scientifically and who taught the world how to sail with guides other than legend. Until Bowditch's time, the maps of the world were great mysteries closely guarded by any captain who had managed to skirt a perilous shore; he was unlikely to give away his secret. For the world to open up, it took the Revolution and such people as Benjamin Franklin, who charted the Gulf Stream, and later Bowditch, who taught lunar navigation. Then Salem men and, in fact, all sailors, were able to move through the seas with greater freedom.

It was almost in the year of Hawthorne's birth that Bowditch, according to a famous story, sailed into Salem harbor in a blinding snowstorm by using his new system of navigation.

There were other great sons of Salem: Samuel McIntire, who had worked first as woodcarver, then made magnificent figureheads and cabin moldings for the ships at sea. It was as an architect that McIntire was to make his name throughout New England. It was he who designed the beautiful houses of Salem—the Peirce-Nichols House, for example—and it was he and his colleagues whose work made for what has been called the finest architectural street in all New England,

Chestnut Street in Salem, where the houses McIntire inspired —the hip-roofed, three-story houses—made architectural history throughout the world.

When Hawthorne was a boy he did not think of architectural history. As with any other boy, it was the sea and the land and Salem's history that interested him most. Probably the death of his father and, later on, two injuries to his foot (the first accident occurred when he was playing ball), deterred Hawthorne from following in that same rolling sailor's gait.

Later, it seemed strange to Hawthorne that Salem began to decline at about the same time his father had died in Surinam. The Salem that interested Hawthorne in later years, the one he was to record with such fascination and insight, was the Salem of the past. He never recorded the seafaring days. That was left to his friend Herman Melville, from New York. But Hawthorne did record the patina of Salem's past. As a young boy, when he wandered the wharves, he could imagine what it had been like in years gone by.

Salem was becoming a place of the past, but a glorious past. Pepper had given way to seal fishing, seal fishing to whaling, and in this Salem had much competition. Nathaniel, as he began to brood about the past, wondered if it was there one should turn one's thoughts if one wanted to write. Not to the present, but to that slightly distant past where the world was shadowy enough to need outline but clear enough so one could create from it an understanding of the present.

Hawthorne was always trying to understand the world around him. A writer always does, but particularly a writer who has had some deep loss, as Hawthorne had had in the death of his father. He was haunted by the past, one might almost say, haunted even as a boy by a curious sense of guilt and discomfort—a common occurrence in a child who has lost a parent. Part of that guilt had been heightened by his mother, who clung so to her household, so frequently disdaining the outside world that she inadvertently put a wall between herself and her children. Despite the fact that she loved her children dearly, she was like one of those Salem houses behind the closed walls, only there was never to be any gate that would open onto her own understanding of her family and herself. Her son, Nathaniel, was to be the exact opposite—so aware of the vagaries and pains of the human heart, so delighted in its pleasures and contentments that, although "stern" upon occasion, as the older Captain Hathorne had been, he could also be a delight and comfort to his friends and family.

The second floor of the Manning home was where the young family settled, but the rest of the house teemed with relatives—aunts and uncles, nieces and cousins. But Nathaniel's own household seemed to be full of women. He longed to talk to men, and sought out the companionship of his uncle, who had an important stage line. In the stables Hawthorne listened to the old stage drivers as they told their stories of journeys through the New England landscape.

Always, like Salem boys before him, he went down to the wharf or perhaps all the way to Juniper Point, or even by foot to Marblehead, or he would walk down the streets and wonder about old Salem society, a society that still existed in Hawthorne's day. The Hawthornes knew their place, of course. After the death of his father, their place was pretty low indeed. And because their family had once been more important, they suffered from the kind of fallen greatness that Hawthorne later thought had afflicted Salem itself.

Salem had another past, a past that was not the sea but that rolled like the sea at high tide. That past was filled with stories and legends you could hear from the old men down at the docks. Hawthorne listened to the local folklore—about the sea monster up at Marblehead, about the woman who was a witch and howled so at home that her husband's ship went down at sea. But mostly he listened to tales of witches and witchcraft.

Hadn't Salem been the home of witches? Hawthorne, walking its streets, looking at those magnificent old houses, wondered what stories they contained. Just as sailors went to sea and wondered about its mysteries, Nathaniel Hawthorne began to captain his own imagination in another way, to steer it in the strange paths of imagination that make a writer. He used to watch those houses and wonder what went on in them, what stories they could tell. Indeed, what story could Salem tell?

The Time of Witches

 2

There . . . listen . . . he could hear the ghosts.

Even as a grown man, Nathaniel Hawthorne used to say he could hear the ghosts in the old houses of Salem—there were many such stories about the old houses and old streets of Salem Village, now Danvers Center, Massachusetts, but in 1692 it was a parish of "old" Salem six miles away. One of the stories that most impressed itself upon Nathaniel Hawthorne's mind as a young boy was Salem's most famous story, the story of the days when it was haunted by witches. Two members of Nathaniel Hawthorne's family were involved in those ancient days of the witch hunts. One was a judge who sat in judgment on the poor souls who were brought before him, and the other was Philip English, who was accused of being under a spell himself.

Everybody believed in witches and charms in those days. The average housewife went out into the dairy, for example, and said the charm, "Come, butter, come," to assure the household of fine butter. Her husband put up marks on the barns to protect his crop from witches and wizards. Witches and wizards also were thought to haunt the sea and to change the direction of the wind so that navigators would lose their way or founder in great waves. Now, in the winter of 1691–1692, a number of things happened that disturbed the people of Salem Village. Crops had been bad for a long time—always considered a sign there were witches in a village. The political and economic independence of Salem itself was shaken. The Massachusetts Bay Colony lost its Charter and there was an emissary in England trying to find out what the future might bring politically to the area. Certainly many early land titles were now in dispute, and the landowners were anxious. There was friction over the most minor problems: heated quarrels as to who should deliver firewood to the ministers, disputes about the boundaries of the neighboring town, embarrassment over the fact that Salem had been publicly reprimanded by the General Court of Massachusetts Bay because of its lack of charity toward the same minister who patiently waited for his firewood. There were also many complex psychological aspects to the hysteria that was about to erupt.

It was a cold winter when Elizabeth, the nine-year-old daughter of Reverend Parris and her cousin Abigail started to do a great deal of shaking. Indeed, they began to shake so hard that it was plain to see they were bewitched.

Anyone could see that Betty, for example, was under some horrible spell. If we look at this spell closely, we can see that she was behaving like a disturbed child trying to get attention. She would stare into space and scream sharply when she was spoken to.

Salem soon followed a witchcraft pattern that had been followed for years in Europe. The hysteria began to spread the way some terrible disease might. A virus of unhappiness and misery was on the land. Soon almost every teen-ager found that she could get a remarkable amount of attention by seeing strange sights or having strange feelings or being unable to listen to prayers. Finally, the doctor, who went down in history as the famous Dr. Griggs, was called and he gave the truth once and for all. His medical diagnosis was: "The evil hand is on them." That was all the community needed; all the misery and hysteria and nervousness that had been stored up in the summer and autumn burst forth during the winter and continued into a terrible spring.

Two magistrates were sent to Salem Village from Salem. One was John Hathorne, Nathaniel Hawthorne's ancestor. It did not enter John Hathorne's head even to question the existence of witches. The Bible said so, and one could not suffer them to live. The books in all the bookcases of the Puritans in those days specifically told how one could deal with witches and where one could find them. There was Baxter's *A Certainty in the World of Spirits*. There was *A Kingdom of Darkness;* and hadn't their own Cotton Mather written his *Memorable Providences?*

Now, if anyone acted curiously in the village, he was brought before the Magistrate. Some were questioned as to why they did not go to church, and they said pathetically that it was because they had no clothes. Truth rarely helped. There was one document that Nathaniel Hawthorne said haunted him for years. It was an examination held in front of the "witch judges," John Hathorne and Jonathan Corwin. This is the document just as it was preserved in the Records of *Salem Witchcraft:*

EXAMINATION BEFORE TRIAL OF
SARAH GOOD.

The examination of Sarah Good before the worshipful Assistants John Hathorne, Jonathan Corwin.

Q. Sarah Good what evil Spirit have you familiarity with?

A. None.

Q. Have you made no contract with the devil?
Good answered no.

Q. Why do you hurt these children?

A. I do not hurt them. I scorn it.

Q. Whom do you employ then to do it?

A. I employ nobody.

Q. What creature do you employ then?

A. No creature but I am falsely accused.

Q. Why did you go away muttering from Mr Parris his house?

A. I did not mutter but I thanked him for what he gave my child.

Q. Have you made no contract with the devil?

A. No.

Many convicted witches were practical, sensible women— Martha Cory, for example, who was a good, law-abiding, prayerful woman who even said, "I am a gospel woman." But what happened? One of the children simply cried out, "She is a gospel witch." And the cries went all through Salem: "Gospel witches, gospel witches—get the gospel witches."

Intelligent people could not believe their ears. Martha Cory said, "We must not believe these distracted children." But the magistrates and those in charge decided not to hear her. They were prey to their own hysteria.

Some of the witches were extremely young; little Dorcas Good, for example, was only five years old. Somebody said she had turned herself into a dog and went around biting people. In addition, there was a poor old woman who had been in bed ill the entire time she was supposed to have gone around the country doing sinful deeds. No one had a defense against such accusations. Anyone could come along and say, "Your shape came to me and bit me last night."

Spring came—the sweet Massachusetts spring—but it brought no sweet feelings. Spring flowered into early May, and Increase Mather, the President of Harvard, came sailing into New England with the new Royal Governor, Sir William Phips. Mather carried a new Charter; this Charter did not meddle with local government, but it did not matter to Salem at that time.

They were conducting their own curious form of democracy. The same teen-age girls who had been making accusations now said that a tall man from Boston was a wizard. Who was he? John Alden, the very John Alden who was the firstborn of John and Priscilla of Plymouth Colony.

Then there was Philip English, one of whose descendants would be Nathaniel Hawthorne. There was a lot of resentment toward English in the Salem of those days. He lived up on Essex Street, in one of the fine houses with many gables. He was a sailor, of course, and had made a great deal of money. The townspeople said you would need more than two hands to tick off the various properties Philip English owned. There was a wharf; a good two dozen ships; more than a dozen buildings. Of course, his very background was suspect because he came from the isolated Isle of Guernsey.

He had done a great deal of muttering as to why he couldn't build a Church of England and worship in the way he had been brought up. That was a treacherous thing to say, and soon he found himself in jail.

Some people began to realize that what they were doing had a kind of insanity about it. One of the men who had gone out to round up witches turned against those who had sent him out and yelled, "Hang them all. They're all witches." So it seemed at the time that all of Salem was under the spell of some evil design.

Years later, the great scholar and specialist in witchcraft, George Kittredge of Harvard, said, "In prosecuting witches, our forefathers acted like other men in the seventeenth century. In repenting and making public confession, they acted like themselves." For we should remember that, although this witchcraft in Salem was a great sore on the early history of our country, our own people made every effort to heal themselves.

Actually, the terrible witchcraft scare in Salem lasted a little less than a year. It is true that twenty people were put to death and two died in jail. In England and Scotland, in earlier trials, hundreds were put to death. Salem, too, righted itself rapidly. People began to see just how wrong they had been. Often the judges and juries recanted and publicly repented. The contemporary Samuel Sewell, who was one of the judges, brooded for years over the Salem tragedy, and he kept a day of fasting and prayer each year in recognition of his mistake.

On the fifteenth of January, 1697, all of Massachusetts made a day of fasting to atone for what they had done to the "witches."

Mr. David R. Proper, one of America's foremost authorities on the Salem witch trials, explains: "Massachusetts was cured of its hysteria and so went on record by clearing the names of those condemned and removing witchcraft from capital offenses before a similar move was taken by any other colony. Witchcraft was not removed from official capital offenses until 1736; and, in fact, the last execution for witchcraft in England took place in 1712, and in Scotland a woman was burned as late as 1727. The sudden and terrible events of 1692 taught America a lesson which today has its application, although the ancient city of Salem will always be associated with the most fantastic misconceptions of witchcraft, when, in reality, Salem's agony is triumph for the dignity of the individual and liberty of all." *

In the meantime, of course, there were those stories of John Hawthorne. His deeds, Nathaniel Hawthorne often said, still rested on the shoulders of his family.

* From *Essex Institute Historical Collections*, Volume C, Number 4.

Five- and Ten-Dollar Schools

❧ 3 ❧

"My Lord, stand back . . . ," Nathaniel would brandish the book he was reading, while his sister Ebe (Elizabeth) looked on. He was nine years old and holding himself carefully; he could barely balance on both feet, one foot now almost useless from an accident that had happened while he was playing ball and bat. He could amuse and delight his older sister nonetheless, and she clapped delightedly as he shouted the line from Richard III, his favorite Shakespeare play.

"My Lord, stand back and let the coffin pass."

Ebe remembered Nathaniel's histrionics all her life and later told Hawthorne's son how his father had curled up in a chair, "reading, reading, reading," or lay flat on the floor surrounded by books that included Paul Bunyan's *Pilgrim's*

Progress, Edmund Spenser's *Faerie Queen,* Thomson's *Castle of Indolence,* and, of course, his beloved Shakespeare.

Ebe herself, had been able to read Shakespeare from the age of six, and her young friend Elizabeth Peabody had shamed her because *she* had first read Shakespeare at four.

Elizabeth Peabody's father had often come to treat Nathaniel's crippled foot. Although Dr. Nathaniel Peabody was a dentist, he was called upon to treat other illnesses, despite the fact that the good doctor was considered by many to be downright radical. He had the ridiculous idea, for example, that many times teeth could be filled instead of pulled.

The Peabodys and the Hawthornes almost shared a common back fence. Ebe Hawthorne went to the school that had been started by Mrs. Peabody, a lady of learning with somewhat elegant airs who told her three daughters, Elizabeth, Mary, and the youngest, Sophia, that they were directly descended from Boadicea, the ancient Queen of the Britons. Elizabeth grew up to be a major force in the history of education in the United States; Mary was to marry the great educator Horace Mann; and Sophia, the youngest, was to marry a brilliant young writer, the boy over the back fence, Nathaniel Hawthorne.

But all this was many years away. For now, the lives of the Hawthornes and the Peabodys were not to be further involved. The Peabody's moved away, while the Hawthornes remained in Salem until Nathaniel Hawthorne was twelve years old. These first twelve years were very important to Nathaniel Hawthorne in his later role as a writer, despite the fact that he had little formal schooling, and the school itself, when he did go, caused him only pain.

Nathaniel couldn't tolerate the laughter of his schoolmates. Once he had been standing ill at ease on the stage of the schoolroom, trying to declaim, in the fashion of the day. He had thought he was doing rather well, but suddenly the large boys crowded into the room and pulled him down from the stage. He was depressed and wretched. Hawthorne always remembered this incident, and it was only many years afterward that he was able to speak well in public.

For many writers school is a painful process. Writers take different paths to discover themselves, and they need more time to do so than many young people who are willing to accept the world as it is. In the world of the writer, this search for identity, as it is called, starts early and continues throughout his life. In the beginning the search always seems to lead the writer to books. He may not be happy in school, but he is generally happy with his books. That same Nathaniel Hawthorne who had been pulled bodily from the school's stage, who had to make himself speak and could not, could, while on his own, even with his bad foot, climb up to the rooftop of his grandfather's house and declaim to the heavens. Walt Whitman, years later, was to walk along Long Island Sound and declaim to the sound of the waves passages from the great books of the world he loved so much.

That was the way to declaim to the world, thought Nathaniel. Climb up on a roof, brace oneself against the chimney and the rooftree, and see all Salem spread out before one—the great activity of Salem port, the graying buildings, the glistening water, iridescent as some of the great passages of literature.

Downstairs were the interior pleasures of a house. Cats, for example. Hawthorne was always devoted to cats, as he was to many animals. And Beelzebub, named after the devil in Milton's "Paradise Lost," was a great creature who used to cuddle near him as he read. Sometimes he would take all the books of the slender library in his home and make a passageway or tunnel for the cats to find their way through—mysterious passages always fascinated Hawthorne and he was later to use them in *The House of the Seven Gables*. Hawthorne's sister Ebe carefully noted through the years Hawthorne's fondness for animals, especially kittens; but he teased them when he was a small boy. His sister warned him that one kitten would never like him again. "Oh, she'll think it was William," he said, blaming his own mischief, as many boys would, on a neighborhood child who played with him.

Years later, Hawthorne's son Julian said that there was a certain mystery in his father's early life. Part of that mystery results from the fact that we have few documents to tell us just what happened. But Julian Hawthorne also meant that there was little to indicate in Nathaniel Hawthorne's boyhood that he would turn out to be one of the great writers of American literature. There is little evidence, in the lives of many boys as to just what direction their destinies will take. As a child, and even as a young man and throughout his life, Julian pointd out, Hawthorne was many-sided and clearheaded. But he was also a man of great energy, and it was surprising that eventually he should settle down to the sedate life of a writer. In later years, his son was angry when a picture of his father began to emerge as a sort of "morbid, timid, milk-and-water 'Frankenstein'."

Elizabeth perhaps understood some of what made their background so useful to a writer. "We always had plenty of books," she said, "and our minds and sensibilities were not unduly stimulated. If he had been educated for a genius, it would have injured him excessively. He developed himself." And that is what young Hawthorne, called "Nath" or "Hath" in those days, did. He developed himself, slowly, quietly, always deepening his imagination, always speculating upon the world, always wondering what could be imagined. "I used to think," he said, "that I could imagine all feelings, all passions, states of the heart and mind."

He knew somehow that he had to protect himself from the outside world, that he was not ready to know it; that by not knowing it too soon, he would be able, when the time came, to know it deeply and well. "One of the peculiarities of my boyhood," he said later, "was a grievous disinclination to go to school. And Providence favoring me in this natural repugnance, I never did go half as much as other boys, partly owing to delicate health, which I made the most of for the purpose, and partly because much of the time there was no school within reach."

We do not know too much about Hawthorne's early schooling, but at one time he remarked that he was now attending a five-dollar school, which was embarrassing because he had first attended a ten-dollar school. He was fortunate, however, in coming near and studying under some great educators of his day, although some might be considered eccentric teachers within the framework of today's educational system. There was Dr. J. E. Worcester, near the Baptist Church on Federal Street in Salem, who took a few intelligent boys. Dr. Worcester had an unusual interest in words and was later to write one of the first American dictionaries.

Evidently the two illnesses in his youth often had kept Nath Hawthorne indoors. Dr. Worcester, for example, came to Nathaniel Hawthorne instead of Hawthorne's going to Dr. Worcester. Undoubtedly there was much discussion between teacher and student about the mystery and beauty of words. The elegance of words was being forgotten— words were simply becoming utilitarian. Dr. Worcester insisted that if you listened to the rich vocabulary of old Salem you would not settle for the less colorful way of speaking that was later to be propagated by Dr. Worcester's Connecticut colleague, Mr. Noah Webster. New England writers were always to hold their Dr. Worcester in esteem and, when his dictionary appeared, Oliver Wendell Holmes rated it as important to New England culture as to rival the Bible.

All of New England at this time had a tremendous interest in learning, and this excitement about letters, more than any actual schooling, was vitally important to Nathaniel Hawthorne. Salem, for example, had fine libraries—one, the Philosophical Library, had started, in true Salem fashion, at sea. Originally the library of a famous Dublin scientist, Dr. Richard Kirwan, it had been seized from a British ship during the Revolution. Later sold at auction, it was purchased by the merchants of Salem. The Salem Atheneum, in which Hawthorne later owned stock, was formed in 1810 by combining, among others, the Social Library and the Philosophical Library. Salem had, too, the famous East India Marine Society—an unusual society that tied Salem to all the corners of the world. Although Nathaniel was never qualified to join, his father had been a member. The qualifications were unusual—you had to be a Salem captain of supercargo who had rounded the Cape of Good Hope or Cape Horn.

Along with this emphasis on the outside world and on learning went emphasis on the private life of reflection, a reflection frequently about Salem's past. Nathaniel Hawthorne shared deeply in this wondering about the past—not only the Salem of the witches but the Salem of the great captains, and even the distant Salem of the Indians.

Salem had been named after the Hebrew word for peace, *Shalom*, when it had first been settled. It was in Salem, they said, that the first town meeting of Massachusetts was held; it was Salem that was the clearinghouse for the great colonial immigration of the seventeenth century; it was in Salem that a ship of three hundred tons was first built—a harbinger of the great port and great shipbuilding center she was to become.

History walked the streets of Salem, and the boy Nathaniel, on his crutches, followed it to the stagecoach-line stables, for example. There he learned the other side of the world of books: the stage-drivers' world of action, of travel, of far places, of folklore. He always got along with simple men, particularly stage drivers, plain sailors, or the crews of the ships he was later to know well in his work in the Custom House offices.

Throughout his life Hawthorne had great affection for a storyteller, and he often used the device of someone telling a story in his books. Some of his first short stories came to him from the stage drivers he knew as a boy. Stage-driving was a great skill in early America; like seafaring, it was an almost hereditary occupation, and many family names were known as stage-driving names. There was a famous Jack Mendom of the Salem mail coach, who, when someone urged him to strike the horses and drive fast, made the memorable comment, "While I drive this coach, I am the whole United States of America." The Potter family, the Ackerman family, the Annables, and Eliots were all famous Salem stage drivers. Occasionally some name from the surrounding country—Patch and Peach, Tather and Blumpy, Tanny and Camp—would appear.

Hawthorne early became familiar with the old roads and the Indian paths that were now the streets of commerce. He was able to imagine what those first faint tracks had been, and he wrote later:

"The forest-track trodden by the hob-nailed shoes of these sturdy and ponderous Englishmen has now a distinctness which it never could have acquired from the light tread of a hundred times as many moccasins. It goes onward from one clearing to another, here plunging into a shadowy strip of woods, there open to the sunshine, but everywhere showing a decided line along which human interests have begun to hold their career. . . . And the Indians coming from their distant wigwams to view the white man's settlement marvel at the deep track which he makes, and perhaps are saddened by a flitting presentiment that this heavy tread will find its way over all the land, and that the wild woods, the wild wolf, and the wild Indian will alike be trampled beneath it."

The sea had changed less than the roads. Down on the Salem docks they might be bringing back sperm oil; slippery and odorous, it left a curious scent in the air. Other packages would contain whalebones to make corset stays for the ladies and whip handles for the men. The stagecoach drivers in the stables always wanted a whalebone whip.

The Salem ships were famous for the whalebone they brought back. The boys who hung around the docks in Salem used to ask the men what they ate on these long trips. "Whale," they would reply. "Men eat whales and Jonah hails those with exultation. It evens things up and plainly brings a due retaliation." And Melville, who was later to meet Hawthorne and to dedicate *Moby Dick* to him, wrote, "In the long dry watches of the night, it is a common thing for seamen to dip their ship biscuit into the huge oil pots and let them fry there for a while. Many a good supper have I made thus."

It is surprising perhaps that Hawthorne never made an attempt to run away to sea; possibly his ill health precluded his having such a thought. He was always disappointed that he had not been able to ship out as a ship's historian in later years when it seemed likely that such a job might be offered him. But down near the docks, barks, brigs, and schooners, he sailed into the world of the imagination.

One must remember that the magic of the sea very distinctly put its mark upon the great writers of that day. It is not perhaps as obvious in Hawthorne's work as it was to be in the work of that greatest mariner-writer of all time, Herman Melville, or even in that of Longfellow, Hawthorne's classmate at college, who wrote of the sea when he said:

"A boy's will is the wind's will,
And the thoughts of youth are long, long thoughts."

Hawthorne's thoughts of youth were long, long thoughts, and although at times he might have been somewhat crippled, his walks were often long and rewarding. If he did not go down to the docks, he would head with his sisters toward Gallow's Hill, famous for the execution of witches, or, better still, seek out that curious prominence known as Folly's Hill, where the towns of Salem, Danvers, and Beverly joined. Hawthorne always loved the area. It was as deserted as a lonely heart and it had succulent berries that you could pop into your mouth while you bent low to protect yourself from the wind. As so many of the houses Hawthorne knew, the one that stood on the hill, called Browne's Folly, had a story.

The house had been built by the Honorable William Browne for his fourteen-year-old bride, Mary Burnet. Browne wanted a magnificent house, a great "folly" of a house, as it was called in those days—too great, too noble for the place in which it was situated. When his wife died soon after her marriage, Browne lost interest in the great cavernous home he had built. After many vicissitudes, it was divided into three houses, and one of them became an old tavern. As a boy, Nathaniel used to go to that long ridge, rising, he said, out of the level country "like a whaleback out of a calm sea."

One of the last things he wrote was about Browne's Folly: "There was one part of the house that everybody was afraid to enter. It seems that an evil spirit, perhaps a domestic demon of the Browne family, was confined in it. One day three or fourscore years ago some schoolboys happened to be playing in the deserted chambers and took it in their heads to develop secrets of this mysterious closet. With great difficulty and tremor, they succeeded in forcing the door. As it flew open, there was a vision of people and garments of antique magnificence—gentlemen in curled wigs and tarnished gold lace, and ladies in brocade and quaint headdresses rushing tumultuously forth and tumbling upon the floor. The urchins took to their heels in huge dismay, but crept back after a while and discovered that the apparition was composed of a mighty pile of family portraits."

Family portraits and apparitions of the past were to haunt Hawthorne, and even one of these great folly houses was to know him intimately. The time came when Mrs. Hawthorne decided to leave Salem, and accordingly the Hawthornes temporarily pulled up stakes for what was then known as the "primeval woods" of Maine.

Amid the Pines of Maine

The stage swayed from side to side as might a staggering, overladen ship in a rough sea. It went along the turnpikes, down country roads, through villages, stopping occasionally at the towns. There the boy Nath preferred the company of the horses and the grooms in the stables. The smell of the stables seemed particularly poignant to him, and the excitement of stagecoach life—everyone always on the move, seeking out some new town, some new village, some new place—fascinated him.

After an enforced rest, his lame leg was better. This freedom was as fresh as the day itself. He was on his way with the rest of his family, traveling always by one of the Manning stagecoaches to Raymond, Maine, to live with his uncle in the great home he had heard about so often. After a while Nath was able to convince the driver to let him sit beside him, and the driver, fond of this boy who had made himself well known around the Manning stables on Herbert Street, allowed him to finish his journey surrounded by scenery and stories—two of the world's pleasures he most enjoyed. As Nathaniel had listened attentively to the stories in Salem, so now he listened to the stories of the road. This interest would continue throughout his life—he had almost a gypsy quality in him. Even in the later years that were known as the years of seclusion, he used to travel incognito, picking up strange stories and tales of the eastern seaboard.

These drivers had many tales to tell about the hazards of the road. Sometimes ghastly mirages (were they ghosts?) would spring up across the road; sometimes great blizzards and storms wreaked havoc on home, hovel, and voyager.

His uncle Richard's house was a great house, like one of those fine houses in Salem that Nathaniel's mother seldom had entered, now that she was a sorry widow. Actually, the house was so grand, so unsuitable for the shores of Lake Sebago on which it was built, that it was called Manning's Folly.

The atmosphere of Raymond was far different from that of Salem. Whereas Salem had an old past that often seemed to stifle the lives of some of its inhabitants, Raymond was a new community—a raw pioneer village that, at least for Nath, opened fresh vistas. Uncle Richard Manning had one of the few necessities of civilization, a store, and stores in those days were meeting places for all the pioneers who purchased supplies and swapped stories with all the gusto with which they breathed the fresh, pine-scented Maine air.

The Manning store was a place of importance. Mrs. Richard Manning was the daughter of old Captain Dingley, one of the first pioneers, for whom Dingley Brook was named.

The Manning House also commanded a view of the road—in one direction, it went off into the wilderness of the Maine woods; in the other, like a finger pointing toward civilization, it carried ox teams, horses, herds of sheep, and travelers to the city of Portland.

It was summer when the Hawthornes first arrived in Maine. Nath stored up many early impressions that came tumbling out in his notebooks during later visits. He was always struck by the giant pines:

"I particularly remarked a stately pine, wholly devoid of bark, rising white in aged and majestic ruin, thrusting out its barkless arms. It must have stood there in death many years ago, its own ghost."

Throughout his life he took time to listen to brooks.

"Above the dam the brook flowed through the forest, a glistening and babbling water-path illuminated by the sun which sent its rays almost straight along its course. It was lovely and wild and peaceful."

Lovely and wild and peaceful—those were the adjectives that best describe Nathaniel Hawthorne's first impressions of Maine. As an adolescent boy, however, it was the wildness that attracted him most.

When Hawthorne was famous in later years he wrote of his happiness in Maine: "I ran quite wild," he said, "and would, I doubt not, have willingly run wild till this time, fishing all day long, or shooting with an old fowling piece; but reading a good deal, too, on the rainy days, especially in Shakespeare and *The Pilgrim's Progress* and any poetry or light books within my reach."

On the opposite side of Dingley Brook across from his own house, Richard Manning later built a house for Elizabeth Hawthorne, and it was there that Nathaniel Hawthorne, his two sisters, and his mother were to spend happy days.

Every little cove and every rock there seemed to hold a story; indeed, Indians had once painted on the nearby cliffs. Nath felt that he was almost an Indian—no longer a child who had been overanxious, perhaps even overprotected; now he was an early adolescent on his own.

He was gone from sunrise to sunset. He met old loggers and heard from them some of the fabulous lumbering lore of the time. He watched oxen pulling loads of timber. He watched river hogs (that is what they called the logmen) branding each log the same way that cattlemen on western ranges branded steers. Each log had its own mark, its own identity. And in those warm summer days in Maine, Nath Hawthorne was beginning to find his.

He had grown away from the women—his sisters and mother, who seemed oppressive at times—and turned instead to two young friends, William Symmes, with whom he could go fishing any day he chose, and his cousin, Jacob Dingley. For the first time in his life, he was not isolated from the group because of his family's love for solitude or his inability to keep up because of his bad foot. In Maine everything seemed all right—friendship as well as his foot—and he skated with "the deep shadows of the icy hills on either hand," he said.

Even his mother seemed happier. Rebecca Manning, her niece, recalled: "I remember Aunt Hawthorne as busy about the house, attending to various matters. Her cooking was excellent and she was noted for a certain kind of sauce which nobody else knew how to make. We always enjoyed going to her when we were children for she took great pains to please us and to give nice things to eat. . . ."

Sometimes Nathaniel was away late into the evening, having lost his way back, perhaps by chance, perhaps because he wanted to sit in one of the log cabins that were often found around Sebago Lake. Always it seemed there was a welcome at the door. Although it might be an empty cabin, a great fire would be waiting. Someone would have left not too long ago; one of those enormous Maine logs would be beckoning the visitor at the door.

Some scholars say that we have a good record of Hawthorne's life at that time because he kept a diary that was later published. Other scholars have disputed the authenticity of the journal. But certainly his life must have been very similar to the one described. His family was to say he always delighted in frightening his friends with ghost stories. The diary records some of the old Maine ghost legends—phantoms inhabiting the old garrets in the house, Devil grounds, where the Devil had once stamped his foot and hundreds of Indians disappeared. The diary contains, too, a history of his friendship with William Symmes, a boy of Afro-American parentage, who had endeared himself to Nath and whom he would never forget. It was probably at this time, too, that Hawthorne met William Pitt Fessenden, the Maine boy who was to become one of State's greatest senators.

Although he learned, as he said, "the cursed habit of solitude," in Maine, he learned a great deal about friendship, too. Fessenden was just one of many great political figures who became Hawthorne's friends, although he had little interest in politics.

Even as a boy in Maine, Hawthorne began to think of himself as a spectator. He stood a little apart from the rest even when he was fishing, even when he was hunting. For one thing, the library of the Mannings was the finest in the pioneer community. Maine had opened two vistas to him— the woods and the human mind. His painful childhood, his ill health, his natural inclinations, his access to and pleasure in books, his ability to be a spectator—one who could look on without losing his humanity or sense of justice—were all keys to the next step in his life.

The Spectator

5

"Salem, Tuesday, September 28, 1819.
"Dear Sister,
    "We are all well and hope you are the same. I do not know
what to do with myself here."
    He was back in Salem again, and, as Nathaniel Hawthorne
wrote the letter to his sister, he was dejected and sorry that
he had left Raymond, Maine, behind him. He continued his
letter, "I shall never be contented here, I am sure. I now go
to a five-dollar school—I that have been to a ten-dollar one.
O Lucifer, son of the morning, how art thou fallen? I wish I
was but in Raymond and I should be happy."
    Raymond began to take on for him a magical quality—it
was the place he had been free. He seemed to sense that he

would never have that freedom again. So often "I would wish for my gun," he would say in a later letter, "and that I could again savagize with you, but I shall never run wild in Raymond and I shall never be as happy as when I did."

Nathaniel Hawthorne was back in Salem to prepare himself for college. He who never liked school was now, as he said, going to a five-dollar school and he was none too happy about it. His sister Louisa, however, whom he had so enjoyed writing to in Maine, returned to Salem in 1820 and the two of them began to enjoy each other's company in a way not possible when both were younger. Nathaniel was often withdrawn with people, but Louisa was gay and lighthearted. She encouraged him to go to a ball. He went, but he seemed far happier with some of their other activities. There was a famous Pin Society that he and his sister founded, and one of his relatives remembered the bound book with blue paper that contained the words:

> "Here are con-
> tained
> The
> Regulations of
> The Pin Society
>   Nathaniel Hawthorne, Secretary, of
>   Salem, Mass. . . ."

It was an exclusive society, and it never contained more than two members, Louisa and Nathaniel, but they discussed the events of the world with great seriousness at their meetings.

Of more importance was *The Spectator*. Nathaniel Hawthorne, who often thought of himself as a spectator, even a Paul Pry, looking upon the affairs of the world from a distance, chose the title *The Spectator* for his first ambitious undertaking, a hand-printed magazine. The name, of course, was based upon the eighteenth-century Addison and Steele *Spectator Papers*, which young Hawthorne so admired.

For the first time, Hawthorne had really put his feet on the path of literature. The wreath of genius was a little top-heavy for his head, but his pen was facile and flowed with the poetry that used to pour out of him.

"I am full of scraps of poetry," he used to complain, "can't keep it out of my brain. I could vomit up a dozen pages more if I were a mind to turn it over." One of the poems went to a Boston newspaper when he was sixteen:

I.

The moon is bright in that chamber fair,
And the trembling starlight enters there
   With a soft and quiet gleam;
The wind sighs through the trees around,
And the leaves send forth a gentle sound,
   Like the voices of a dream.

II.

He has laid his weary limbs to sleep;
But the dead around their vigil keep,
   And the living may not rest.
There is a form on that chamber floor
Of beauty which should bloom no more,—
   A fair, yet fearful guest!

III.

The breath of morn has cooled his brow,
And that shadowy form has vanished now,
   Yet he lingers round the spot;
For the pale, cold beauty of that face,
And that form of more than earthly grace,
   May be no more forgot.

IV.

There is a grave by yon aged oak,
But the moss-grown burial-stone is broke
   That told how beauty faded;
But the sods are fresh o'er another head,
For the lover of that maiden dead
   By the same tree is shaded.

This poem is a little better than are most of adolescence, but not much better. There was nothing in Hawthorne's adolescent fascination with words that assured the genius of his later works.

When he wasn't writing poetry, he very carefully concentrated on his magazine, *The Spectator*. It was filled with his own particular sense of humor, a very delightful family trait. In the "Wanted" column appeared, "Wanted: a husband, not above 70 years of age, none need apply unless they can produce good recommendations or are possessed of at least $10,-000. The applicant is young, being under 50 years of age and of great beauty. Mary Manning, Spinstress." That was his Aunt Mary. She probably didn't appreciate Nath's efforts on her behalf.

The magazine, all of its seven issues, seems to have been enjoyed very much by the Hawthorne family. Occasionally there is a statement that makes us realize we *are* dealing with the boyhood of a writer. At one point Hawthorne says, "Nathaniel Hathorne proposes to publish by Subscription a NEW EDITION of the MISERIES OF AUTHORS, to which will be added a SEQUEL containg [sic] FACTCS [sic] and REMARKS drawn from his own experience."

The nature of the artist was something that would concern Hawthorne all his life, and one could tell that even now, young as he was, he was beginning to be a spectator of his own soul and talent.

His pleasantest time was spent in what he called "The Spectator Printing Office, No. 2 Herbert Street, up two pairs of stairs," the very room in which he would write his way to fame. As a matter of fact, he was to say later, "In this dismal chamber, fame was won."

But fame was far from him. As a matter of fact, just the business of being further educated was the problem of the moment. He was being tutored for college by the famous Salem lawyer Benjamin L. Oliver. He continued to read the books he loved so much, *The Faerie Queen,* which was the first book he bought with his own money (he would name his first daughter Una after the heroine in *The Faerie Queen*); *The Pilgrim's Progress,* which was ever present with him, as though in part he were trying to progress through his own adolescence by that rich guide of the eighteenth century.

Nathaniel Hawthorne's letters were delightful, and one remains that he wrote to his mother before he started for college in Maine. It is a letter that tells us a great deal about Hawthorne, even to the career he was about to undertake. It shows his love and affection for his family, his sense of humor, and the beginning of a dedication that was to remain with him all his life. Here is part of it:

"Salem, March 13, 1821"
"Dear Mother,
    ". . . What has become of Elizabeth? Does she never intend to notice me again? I shall begin to think she has eloped with some of those 'gay deceivers' who abound in Raymond, if she does not give me some proof to the contrary. I dreamed the other night that I was walking by the Sebago;

and when I awoke was so angry at finding it all a delusion, that I gave Uncle Robert (who sleeps with me) a most horrible kick.

"I don't read so much now as I did, because I am more taken up in studying. I am quite reconciled to going to college, since I am to spend the vacations with you. Yet four years of the best part of my life is a great deal to throw away. I have not yet concluded what profession I shall have. The being a minister is out of the question. I should not think that even you could desire me to choose so dull a way of life. Oh, no, mother, I was not born to vegetate forever in one place, and to live and die as calm and tranquil as—a puddle of water. As to lawyers, there are so many of them already that one half of them (upon a moderate calculation) are in a state of actual starvation. A physician, then, seems to be 'Hobson's choice'; but yet I should not like to live by the diseases and infirmities of my fellow-creatures. And it would weigh very heavily on my conscience, in the course of my practice, if I should chance to send any unlucky patient 'ad inferum,' which being interpreted is, 'to the realms below.' Oh that I was rich enough to live without a profession! What do you think of my becoming an author, and relying for support upon my pen? Indeed, I think the illegibility of my hand-writing is very author-like. How proud you would feel to see my works praised by the reviewers, as equal to the proudest productions of the scribbling sons of John Bull. But authors are always poor devils, and therefore Satan may take them. I am in the same predicament as the honest gentleman in 'Espriella's Letters,'—

" 'I am an Englishman, and naked I stand here,
A-musing in my mind what garment I shall wear.'

"But as the mail closes soon, I must stop the career of my pen. I will only inform you that I now write no poetry, or anything else. I hope that either Elizabeth or you will write to me next week.

"I remain

"Your affectionate son,
"Nathl. Hawthorne

"Do not show this letter."

College Days

 6

"Left, right. Left, right." The marching continued even in the damp mist of a May morning in Maine. "Pick up your feet. Pick up your feet. Left, right. Left, right."

The early morning made the boys' legs drag. They never seemed to get enough sleep at college. These were the self-appointed "cadets" of Bowdoin College, Brunswick, Maine. Bowdoin was a young college with young ideals. It had been established in the very early years of the nineteenth century. When its first class graduated in 1806, there were just seven members. The "cadets" were a group of Bowdoin college boys dressed in homespun clothes, carrying on their shoulders branches from the pine trees that they had picked up from the ground.

One of the officers was Franklin Pierce. He would become President of the United States one day, but it hardly seemed likely now as the mist curled his hair farther beneath his cap. He would know, too, what it would truly mean to be a general and would fight magnificently in the Mexican War. But here, on what was called the Parade Ground, his cadets were a sorry sight. Two in particular seemed to stand a little apart from the rest. One, Private Henry Wadsworth Longfellow; the other, Private Nathaniel Hawthorne.

Pierce and Hawthorne were good friends and would continue to be so for the rest of their lives. But, during their college days, all three were trying to show their respect for a belief, for a cause. They all admired Lord Byron, who had gone to support the Greeks in their war against the Turks.

Hawthorne had read Byron's "Childe Harold" and declaimed its words over the rooftops of Salem; now, as a young man, he began to explore the meanings behind the words and the meaning of freedom.

A new idea of freedom was being fostered by Byron's struggle in Greece. And the boys at Bowdoin, thousands of miles away, had decided to set up a military company. Who knows? Perhaps they, too, would go to Greece and fight nobly. None of them did.

Those Bowdoin students, however, were an unusual group. They went on to live lives of great importance to their families and to their country and—as far as Longfellow and Hawthorne were concerned—to the great universe of letters.

Henry Wadsworth Longfellow, as did Nathaniel, had Pilgrim blood in his veins. Like Nathaniel, he, too, had Revolutionary heroes for his ancestors. He had been born in Portland, Maine, on February 27, 1807, while it still was a part of the Commonwealth of Massachusetts. He had roamed the Maine's wilderness as had Nathaniel and knew the ferment of the seaport towns that inspired so many writers of the period.

Longfellow and Hawthorne did not share the rare intimacy that existed between Hawthorne and Pierce, but they were good and steadfast friends throughout the years. It was Hawthorne who gave Longfellow the magnificent idea for his poem "Evangeline"; it was Longfellow who delivered the beautiful tribute to Hawthorne upon his death, given in the concluding chapter of this book.

Longfellow was more prolific at the beginning of his literary career, but they published their first single poems almost simultaneously as teen-agers. Longfellow's was attacked as being too "stiff," and this attack made him call critics "alligators"—a reference very much enjoyed by his friends. For his part, Longfellow was always a sympathetic critic, and his appreciation for Nathaniel started early and continued throughout Hawthorne's writing career. He praised Hawthorne's *Twice-Told Tales* and then said later that Hawthorne's *The Scarlet Letter* was pre-eminent among works of American fiction, and that *The House of the Seven Gables* had even "a greater diversity of power." When he read *The Marble Faun*, his eyes were not as strong as they had been and it was his practice to avoid night reading. But his friend's "magical faun and magical pen" changed all that. He nearly blinded himself, he said, reading it rapidly one night, and he wrote to a friend a description of Hawthorne's work that is as fresh today as when it was written. Hawthorne, he said, "always sees everything in that magical twilight atmosphere where fact merges into fable. . . . His story has the same painful tone, deeper even than a minor key, which all his books have, as if written by a fallen angel. . . ."

Nathaniel Hawthorne, in one of the stagecoaches he so enjoyed, had arrived in Bowdoin in the fall of 1821. Franklin Pierce had been one of the passengers in the same carriage, but there were others: Jonathan Cilley and Alfred Mason, who was to be Hawthorne's first roommate. During the entire trip Nath was in a state of nervous anxiety. He had never really properly been in school, so how could he hope to pass the entrance examination? During the whole journey, his uncle wrote to his mother, "he was doubtful."

He had no need to be. He did pass his examinations, but for a while it looked as though he would be no better a student in college than he had been in school. "I was an idle student," he said, "negligent of college rules . . . rather choosing to nurse my fancies than to dig into Greek roots and be numbered among the learned Thebans."

His friend, Horatio Bridge, has told us what Nath liked about college and what he disliked. "He disliked mathematics and metaphysics, but he did like languages," said Bridge, "especially did he like Latin, which he wrote with great ease and purity. In the other studies of the curriculum he stood hardly above mediocrity, and in declamation he was literally nowhere. He never declaimed in the old chapel as the students were required to do on Wednesday. Fines and admonitions were powerless; he would not declaim." He would not declaim in public because of his embarrassment and discomfort when he had been pulled off the stage as a very young boy.

Oratory was important in the Bowdoin of those days, but so were other things. It was a miniature Harvard, a rural Harvard—Brunswick was a place of unpainted fences and sandy yards, with cows roaming the streets. Men with wheelbarrows as well as students made up the campus scene.

All around was Maine, the great and glorious silence of her forests, the rush and quiet beauty of her waters, in which the boys took such delight in fishing.

They studied Murray's *English Grammar* and Blair's *Rhetoric*. They studied nothing, however, of the history of Europe and very little of the history of their own country.

They kept stringent rules. One could not sing loudly in college or shout or clap one's hands. One must be in one's room Saturday and Sunday evenings and abstain from diversions of every kind. The law said that those who violated the Sabbath by any "unnecessary business, visiting or receiving visits or by walking abroad or by any amusement or in any other ways, may be admonished or suspended." And of course there was to be no card-playing or billiards, and one could not go off shooting or fishing without explicit permission.

But there was much card-playing, nevertheless, and every boy at one time or another went shooting and fishing.

The college bell rang early each morning, and first one had to attend chapel. It was colder than the coldness of the Puritan. "College was all right," said Nathaniel when he wrote home. He had friends and he grew less homesick.

By that time, his son Julian wrote later, he was the handsomest young man of his day in that part of the world. "Such is the report of those who knew him, and there is a miniature of him taken some years later which bears out the report. He was five feet ten and one-half inches in height, broad-shoulders but of a light athletic build, not weighing more than one hundred and fifty pounds. His limbs were beautifully formed and the molding of his neck and throat was as fine as anything in antique sculpture. His hair was in a long curving wave and it approached blackness in color. His head was large and grandly developed. His eyebrows were dark and heavy with a superb arch and space between. His nose was straight, but the contour of his chin was Roman. His eyes were large, dark blue, brilliant, and full of varied expression." People were to comment throughout his life that they had never known such eyes as those of Nathaniel Hawthorne. Bayard Taylor used to say they flashed fire. Charles Reade said that he had never seen such eyes in a human head.

Years later, when Hawthorne was in England and Scotland, his glance was compared to the piercing gaze of Robert Burns, and there is a story that, while he was still in college, an old gypsy woman met him once on a woodland path, gazed at him, and asked, "Are you a man or an angel?"

He was no angel. As a matter of fact, he was far from it. He was having a great deal of difficulty adapting to college at all. He had been free to roam as he pleased. Now he felt under restrictions. He played cards and sometimes, instead of being quiet, he gave vent to high spirits or to a rage that would have quelled a crew of mutinous privateersmen at least as effectively as did Bold Daniel, his grandfather. "His voice was then not a bellow but it had the searching electrifying quality of the blast of a trumpet."

The card-playing caused a bevy of letters between President Allen of Bowdoin and Mrs. Hawthorne. "Madame," said one of the President's letters, of May 29, 1821, "by vote of the Executive Government of this college, it is made my duty to request your cooperation with us in the attempt to induce your son faithfully to observe the laws of this institution. He was this day fined fifty cents for playing cards for money the last term. He played at different times. Perhaps he might not have gamed, were it not for the influence of a student, whom we have dismissed from college. It does not appear that your son has very recently played cards; yet your advice may be beneficial to him."

That letter annoyed Hawthorne, and he was eager to set the story straight with his mother. He did not try to dissemble. He wrote to his mother on May 30:

"My dear Mother,
"I hope you have arrived safely in Salem. I have nothing particular to inform you of, except that all the Card Players in college have been found out, and my unfortunate self

among the number. One has been dismissed from college, two suspended, and the rest, with myself, have been fined 50 cents each. I believe the President intends to write to the friends of all the delinquents. Should that be the case, you must show the letter to nobody. If I am again detected, I shall have the honor of being suspended. When the President asked what we played for, I thought it proper to inform him it was 50 cts. although it happened to be a quart of wine, but if I had told him of that he would probably have fined me for having a blow. There was no untruth in the case, as the wine cost 50 cts. I have not played at all this term. I have not drank [sic] any kind of spirit or wine this term, and I shall not till the last week. P.S. I must have some money, for I have none left except about 75 cts. Do not show this."

Later he wrote this further comment to his mother: "The President's message is not so severe as I expected. I perceive that he thinks I have been lead [sic] away by the wicked ones; in which, however, he is greatly mistaken. I was full as willing to play as the person he suspects of having inticed [sic] me, and would have been influenced by no one. I have a great mind to commence playing again, merely to show him that I scorn to be seduced by another into anything wrong."

Letters from Hawthorne's sophomore year tell us less about what he was thinking and doing, but there is one document extant that is extremely interesting today. It is a college bill for the year 1823:

"For tuition	$8.00
Chamber rent	3.34
Damages	.45
Average Damages	.15
Sweeping and Bedmaking	1.11
Library	.50
Monitor	.05

Catalogues	.08
Bell	.11
Renting room	.25
Chemical lectures	.25
Fines	.20

$14.49"

Uncle Robert Manning was still paying for Hawthorne's education. Before college, the boy had worked as a secretary for the livery stable, for $1.00 a week, and it was expected that he would join the Manning Stage Line on graduation.

As with many young men, Nath was disturbed that his family would expect too much from him or, worse still, the wrong kind of future. When one of his relatives encountered him in Brunswick, he sent word back to Salem that Nathaniel was truly exceptional. Nath was upset and wrote home, "I am not very well pleased with Mr. Dike's report of me. The family had before conceived much too high an opinion of my talents, and probably formed expectations which I shall never realize. I have thought much upon the subject and have finally come to the conclusion that I shall never make a distinguished figure in the world, and all I hope or wish is to plod along with the multitude. I do not say this for the purpose of drawing any flattery from you but merely to set Mother and the rest of you right, upon a point where your partiality has led you astray. I did hope that Uncle Robert's opinion of me was nearer the truth, as his deportment toward me never expressed a very high estimation of my abilities."

A few papers from Hawthorne's college years survive, and they were shown at the dedication of the Nathaniel Hawthorne-Henry Wadsworth Longfellow Library at Bowdoin College in 1966. One delightful document was Hawthorne's copy of the "Laws of Bowdoin College," upon which he had scribbled and doodled in true school fashion; another is the handwritten Constitution of the Potato Club,—(Pot)–8–o— a dining club blessing the Maine potato and friendship.

One of the members of the Potato Club, David Shipley, became a famous Congregational minister, and he left a record of Hawthorne in college. ". . . he utterly neglected many of the studies of the regular course; and, as he would not study, he could not at recitations show the fruit of his study. Failure in the classroom, however, did not disturb him; nor did it materially detract from the respect in which he was held, both by professor and classmates. It was soon found that he was not to be judged or dealt with by ordinary standards; that he had read much; that his mind was enriched by its own creations; that he was, in a sense, already an accomplished scholar. In the social circle his was apt to be a silent presence; but it was a presence ever eagerly sought, and, somehow, marvellously magnetic. He never seemed to think of asking himself how he compared with his fellows. In their thoughts he was always above and never beneath. He was near, yet distant; had intimacies, but intimates knew him only in part. In subsequent life, in reference to a certain locality in England, he writes, 'Here a man does not seem to consider what other people will think of his conduct, but only whether it suits his own convenience to do so and so.' And he adds, 'This may be the better way.' When he was in college, he may have seemed to be of the mind here indicated; only it never suited his convenience to do anything with which his associates were not obstinately bent on being pleased. He had no liking for any of the professions, and, it is probable, left college without any definite plans for life."

Hawthorne did have some definite idea, however; he seemed to be sure now that he wanted to be a writer. His sister wrote, "It was in college that he formed the design of becoming an author by profession. In a letter to me he says that he had 'made progress on my novel.' " (Critics are not sure if this was his first published novel *Fanshawe;* his sister often gave different dates for the same undertaking.)

There seems to have been a feeling of impatience in Nath during his senior year at college. He was often without enough funds; his clothes were frequently too thin for Maine's coldness. (The Mannings did not believe in extravagance.) A letter of August 11, 1824, shows in a post script this "terrible hurry."

"My Dear Louisa,

"My want of decent clothes will prevent my calling at Mrs. Sutton's. Write immediately, write immediately, write immediately.

"Haste, haste, post-haste, ride and run, until these shall be delivered. You must and shall and will do as I desire. If you can think of a true excuse, send it; if not, any other will answer the same purpose. If I do not get a letter by Monday, or Tuesday at farthest, I will leave Brunswick without liberty."

Graduation in 1825 was marked by a speech by Longfellow entitled "Our Native Writers." "Already has a voice," he said, "been lifted up in this land, already a spirit and a love of literature are springing up in the shadows of our free political constitution."

Nathaniel nodded his head as if he knew his was to be one of the strongest, richest voices.

New England's literary history, which indeed is really the beginning of all the literary history of the United States, had two great flowerings. Samuel Eliot Morison, the great historian of the American people and particularly of early New England, has pointed out that there was a "little flowering" that eventually became what the critic Van Wyck Brooks, in the title of his book called *The Flowering of New England.*

The later flowering was the Golden Age of American litera-
ture, and one of the figures in that Golden Age was to be
Nathaniel Hawthorne. His friends Herman Melville and
Henry Wadsworth Longfellow, his neighbors Ralph Waldo
Emerson, Henry Thoreau, Dr. Oliver Wendell Holmes,
James Russell Lowell, Margaret Fuller, Charles A. Dana,
Bronson Alcott—all these names were to be intertwined with
Hawthorne's own life. They were to be either intimates,
neighbors, travelers, or fellow members of literary clubs.

It was the spirit of the time that mattered. If, in 1776, there
had been what was called "The spirit of '76," symbolized by
the trio of drummer, fifer, and flag-bearer, the age of Hawthorne was the "spirit of great letters," symbolized by its
books.

Dr. Nathaniel Bowditch of Salem said, "We are living in
the best days of the republic," and certainly by the time
Hawthorne was graduated from Bowdoin, this seemed very
true. It was less true in Salem, whose great seafaring days
were waning by the time of the War of 1812, but it was
certainly true in nearby Boston and in Cambridge.

Although Hawthorne was isolated from the intellectual
ferment of Cambridge and Boston immediately after his
graduation from school, he was not nearly as isolated as he
thought. Salem itself teemed with intense literary and intellectual spirit. It had great magazines: for example, *The
North American Review*, under George Bancroft. Van
Wyck Brooks described this sudden bursting of literary
vigor in New England in the following way: "The New
England imagination had been roused by the tales of travel-
lers and the gains of commerce. The revival of ancient learning, the introduction of modern learning, the excitements of
religious controversy, after the long winter of Puritanism,
spring had come at last, and the earth reappeared in its
beauty."

The United States had never properly appreciated itself as a literary center. The good writers, it was still thought, came from Europe; there was really no American poetry. Once, when Professor Edward Tyrrel Channing and his cousin, Richard Henry Dana, who was to sail for two years before the mast and write one of the great adventure books of all times, were traveling in a stage from Cambridge to Boston, they read a poem by a very young man who lived in the Berkshires. His name was William Cullen Bryant, and the poem was "Thanatopsis." "That was never written on this side of the water," said Dana. But he was wrong. The new age of American letters had begun.

There was a tremendous interest in history. Men who had fought during that other age of a great spirit, the Spirit of '76, were still alive, and the tales they told were known to all. Lexington and Concord, Marblehead and Plymouth, Salem and Boston—all were landmarks of the great historic trail that led to the heart of American literature.

Each of the writers of Hawthorne's day was familiar, as he himself was, with the deep feeling of the past. They all knew something about that first flowering of New England that had occurred shortly after their ancestors arrived from England.

Those very early men, had played many different roles. They were writers and scientists, educators and ministers, lawyers and politicians. They were artists and adventurers. They were such people as John Winthrop, one of the first Americans to be asked to join the British Royal Society, the famous scientific organization. He brought a library of a thousand volumes to Massachusetts in 1631. That library is now the basis of the New York Society Library.

Winthrop's reputation as a scientist was so widespread that by the time he died it was said he had discovered that magical essence, the philosopher's stone, which alchemists and scientists had been seeking for hundreds of years. Winthrop and many other scientists of those years were concerned with magic, with old "simples," with cures that were so often speculated upon in Hawthorne's own books.

There was John Eliot, apostle to the Indians. There was the first major woman writer, Mistress Anne Bradstreet— "the tenth muse," she was called. There was a great craftsman of Boston, John Hull, who was the very first of the colonial artists, and then there were all whose names appeared in the history books and documents of the period—names with which Hawthorne would familiarize himself in the years to come.

This was the first flowering of New England—little buds on the great stalk of the continent itself. The flowering blossomed in many ways—in homes and in villages; in the very creation of systems of government; in libraries. It spread into books and to printing.

Schools were formed, colleges established. If the very small amount Hawthorne paid for his college years seems strange, remember he was only a few generations away from the colonial colleges, where tuition was paid with pork and wheat and corn and meal, or with cotton and lace. The quarter of a year's tuition at Harvard in the seventeenth century cost a bushel of wheat. If you were particularly fortunate and had a little brown cow, you might even have all your beds made and a den for a study for half a year. One young man by the name of Zachary Brigden was fortunate in acquiring an enormous hog of sixty-three pounds that he exchanged for food and drink during his entire first term.

Casks of butter or barrels of salt beef,—the kind of payment did not matter. The important thing was education, and New England loved education. Whether in a cottage or in a larger house, the talk was of the great books of the past, of the great Latin writers Cicero and Virgil, of the Greek giants, Homer and Hesiod. There wasn't a school that didn't teach and encourage reading.

Of course, it was a small area of the world. At the end of the seventeenth century, the New England colonies contained only 106,000 people. Boston had only about 7,000 citizens. But every home had a library, however meager. There was always a large Bible and a small one. We know some of the books owned by persons whose names are familiar. We know that Miles Standish, for example, owned Caesar's *Commentaries*. But even in that first flowering, Americans were recording their own history: *Of Plymouth Plantation*, by Governor Bradford; *New England's Memoriall*, by Nathaniel Morton of Plymouth, Massachusetts; *New England Prospect*, by William Wood. Nathaniel Hawthorne was early familiar with *New England Prospect*. In effect, much of the writing he was to do was to be such a prospect itself, a picture of New England, but a New England of the soul and of the mind and of the deepest literary significance.

It is important to know a little about the early flowering of New England because it throws much light on the later flowering of Hawthorne's own talent. He used stories of colonial New England as a jumping-off point for his great talent. Some of the most penetrating writers of the world have used such a limited framework, within which to express themselves fully on another level. James Joyce, for example, took just a single day in the history of Dublin, his native city, about which to write one of the great books of the twentieth century, *Ulysses*. Herman Melville took just one trip, the trip of the whaler "Pequod," as a springboard for a masterpiece of the nineteenth century, *Moby Dick*. Nathaniel Hawthorne, in many ways, took his part of the country and gave it to the world.

His own village, Salem, was almost the heart of his work. Randall Stewart, one of the great editors and critics who "rediscovered" Hawthorne's richness for our own century, has written: "Hawthorne said that New England was about as large a lump of this earth as his heart could readily take in."

Back in Salem after the years at Bowdoin, he retreated for a while to the room under the eaves, as he called it. There he began to reflect upon what he would do and how he could best explore his own "lump of earth."

The Room Under the Eaves

7

"Mr. Hawthorne's manuscript awaits his orders."

There was nothing else to do now, Hawthorne felt, but to burn the manuscript. All the doubts a young writer feels about his work—half pride, half trepidation—dogged Nath's early efforts at writing. Just as James Joyce, one of the great geniuses of Irish letters, was to suffer endlessly in an effort to find his first publisher, so did Nathaniel Hawthorne. A young printer in Salem was finally persuaded to publish a manuscript entitled *Seven Tales of My Native Land*, but he delayed so long that Nath, in the sudden despair and rage that often trouble young writers, did what he felt he must do. Very deliberately, he burned every page. Curiously, years later, James Joyce was to do exactly the same thing with his first important manuscript.

"What is more potent than fire?" Hawthorne asked in his story, "The Devil in Manuscript," a story that reflects Hawthorne's own efforts as a writer.

"All that I had accomplished," cries out Oberon in that story (Oberon, a character in Shakespeare's *A Midsummer Night's Dream*, was a name bestowed upon Hawthorne himself by some of his college friends), "all that I had accomplished, all that I planned for future years, has perished by one common ruin and left only this heap of embers."

The same story shows, too, the continued anguish of a young writer trying to place his work. In it, seventeen publishers had rejected Oberon's stories, for varying and depressing reasons.

"It would make you stare to read their answers . . . one man publishes nothing but school-books; another has five novels already under examination . . . another gentleman is just giving up business on purpose, I verily believe, to escape publishing my book. . . . But there does seem to be one honest man among these seventeen unrighteous ones; and he tells me fairly that no American publisher will meddle with any American work, seldom if by a known writer, and never if by a new one unless at the writer's risk."

These are revealing words regarding the state of publishing in America in the early part of the nineteenth century. The bookseller and the publisher were one and the same man, unlike the situation today, in which the roles are separated. "Literature" was held in suspicion. Juveniles, textbooks, and religious publications made up the bulk of publishing; the rest, a small ten percent, included what was called "literature"—novels, essays, poems, and so on, and many of these were of European origin. Although all of America was on the verge of a great literary awakening, one of its leading figures, Nathaniel Hawthorne, spent nearly a dozen years in deep creative anguish, almost living the life of a recluse in the room under the eaves in the house on Herbert Street in Salem.

For the rest of his life it seemed he would try to dodge his birthplace, the place where he had such extraordinary roots. But his sister Elizabeth said, "By some fatality we all seem to be brought back to Salem in spite of our intentions and even resolutions." Years later, Hawthorne wrote, "Though invariably healthy elsewhere, there is within me a feeling for old Salem which in lack of a better phrase I must be content to call affection."

But there seemed to be no affection for Salem when he returned from college. His were the usual feelings of a young man leaving college and about to set off on his own paths. Only, for Hawthorne, all the paths seemed to lead inevitably to the same spot, to the sleepy town of Salem, to the town that had once been great but now was far less than great— where the weeds grew in ancient fields and the dust collected in once-lavish rooms and the wharves were crumbled and rotten with time and neglect.

Everyone was vaguely annoyed with him: his uncle Manning, because he had declined to go into the stagecoach business and instead picked up the ridiculous idea of having a literary career; his mother, because he did not always give her the proper respect for her continuing grief; his sisters, because he seemed to rule the roost despite the fact that he sequestered himself most of the day in the room under the eaves.

It was a wonderful room—it was Hawthorne's refuge, study, home, hearth. It held all his hopes, all his dreams, all his desires. And yet for a while these were all in a jumble— the way a young man's room is—never too tidy, too much in disarray, with an air of bewildered confusion. His thoughts were perhaps a little like this, as they are with all writers who must single out the important strains in their life's work, the way women sort children's clothes in a drawer. Some clothes still fit, some do not. What were the clothes of literature that would suit him for the rest of his life?

He was very sure of what he wanted to do. He was like many great writers who make their plans early and persevere. He wanted to be a writer, but what did being a writer mean in the early part of the nineteenth century? A new type of American writing was evolving. But in Salem one could not be quite sure what turn the wind of literature would take. Would it come roaring out of the northeast like a great storm from the waters that surrounded New England? Yes, it might. In fact, it did. One of the greatest stories of all time, Herman Melville's *Moby Dick,* was shaped from the storm and mist of oceans and ancient whale ships fighting the elements, both of which so haunted Hawthorne's youth.

Would the new literature come from the world of the Indians? Hawthorne often brooded about this and never could quite understand how literature could be made from that primitive world. It was true, of course, that he had wanted to be an Indian as a boy—most boys do—but to make a literature of this was something he thought was impossible, though James Fenimore Cooper was to do just that.

Would the new literature come from the folklore of the country whose roots and purpose Hawthorne's people were just beginning to understand? Suddenly these stories seemed far more important than the dusty stories of Europe that had so ruled the literature of the New World. Were there not stories in the hollows of the hills? Were there not stories of the devil visiting the Puritan past? Were there not great legends that had never been explained—the carbuncle in the hills, for example?

He sat at his desk and wondered. One can understand why

he had been called Oberon at school, for there was in Hawthorne a kind of other-worldly quality. He was unusually
handsome. He had the regal head of some old sea captain, but
with dark curly hair that was his sisters' pride. He had great
strength. He could leap shoulder high (he was no longer
troubled with lameness), they said, and in the streets of
Salem late at night you might see what appeared to be a sailor
going down the streets with a strange, loping, sailor's walk,
but it was really Hawthorne.

During the day he avoided going out, as did most other
members of the Hawthorne family, but frequently he
walked at night. Often he slipped out of the house and went
down to Juniper Point. There he would reflect at the shore
of the sea, noticing different seaweeds that had been driven
in by a storm. He would pick up the eel grass, bundling it up
in his hands. He would bend over to examine the bits of
painted wood from long-ruined ships and the bark that had
become enmeshed in the long pounding of sea and sand. As always, the things that were old appealed to him—the juniper
trees, decayed and moss-grown; the grass rotting beside
them.

Sometimes he would walk late in the afternoon on a summer day toward Beverly. There, when no one was about, he
would bathe in a cove sheltered by maple and walnut trees.
Often he would run across a group of small girls who always
were startled to see this strange young man, with his great
mop of hair, walking quietly along pasture paths. He liked to
watch his own shadow cast by the sun.

Sometimes he took one of the Manning stagecoaches and
went to Boston—always, as he used to say, "incognito."
There he visited the taverns where the theatre folk were half
asleep in their chairs, or went into oyster shops or down to
the steamboat wharves at Nahant to watch the passengers
land.

He steadily kept his notebook, jotting down passing scenes or passing thoughts:

"On the common, at dusk, after a salute from two field-pieces, the smoke lay long and heavily on the ground, without much spreading beyond the original space over which it had gushed from the guns. It was about the height of a man. The evening clear, but with an autumnal chill."

"The world is so sad and solemn, that things meant in jest are liable, by an overpowering influence, to become dreadful earnest,—gayly dressed fantasies turning to ghostly and black-clad images of themselves."

"A story, the hero of which is to be represented as naturally capable of deep and strong passion, and looking forward to the time when he shall feel passionate love, which is to be the great event of his existence. But it so chances that he never falls in love, and although he gives up the expectation of so doing, and marries calmly, yet it is somewhat sadly, with sentiments merely of esteem for his bride. The lady might be one who had loved him early in life, but whom then, in his expectation of passionate love, he had scorned."

"The scene of a story or sketch to be laid within the light of a street-lantern; the time, when the lamp is near going out; and the catastrophe to be simultaneous with the last flickering gleam.

"The peculiar weariness and depression of spirits which is felt after a day wasted in turning over a magazine or other light miscellany, different from the state of the mind after severe study; because there has been no excitement, no difficulties to be overcome, but the spirits have evaporated insensibly."

The Room Under the Eaves

They said there were ghosts in the yard of the Hawthorne house at Herbert Street, and certainly in those early notebooks the supernatural often rears its head: "In an old house a mysterious knocking might be heard on a wall where had formerly been a doorway now bricked up," or then a thought that haunted him more and more when he felt that he should get away from Salem but seemed unable to move: "A person even before middle age may become musty and faded among the people with whom he has grown up from childhood, but by migrating to a new place he appears fresh with the effect of youth which may be communicated from the impressions of others to his own feelings."

He read constantly—all the histories of Maine and Massachusetts that he could put his hands on: Felt's famous *Annals of Salem* and the *History of Haverell*. He read hungrily, as though he were trying to get the past to tell its story. He went to the museums, looked at the old portraits, wondered about what they had to say. If one only knew one could unravel the entire history of our New World.

When he did not look at portraits of others he sometimes looked entranced at what he saw in a mirror. The mirror haunted many of his stories. It reflected each of the tales of the Pyncheons in *The House of the Seven Gables* and, in those early years, as he learned his craft, he wrote in his notebook that one could "make one's own reflection in the mirror the subject of a story," and the same year he noted, "follow out the fantasy of a man taking his life by installments instead of at one payment, say ten years of life alternately with ten years of suspended animation."

That appeared to be what Hawthorne was doing—living for the moment in a state of suspended animation. But his ten years were turned to twelve before he really shook the spirit of alienation, differentness that he had allowed to sink over him in those apprentice years.

Each writer chooses a different way to be an apprentice. He does not always know at the time quite what he is doing, and Hawthorne seemed to work at his craft far more consciously than many other writers. Melville went to sea, felt the grease and slipperiness of the whaleship's deck under his feet; he said the whaleship was his Yale and Harvard College.

Some simply traveled, extending their college years indefinitely as they wandered over the European scene. Longfellow went to spots that were then unfamiliar to most Americans: Germany and Scandinavia.

Everyone seemed suddenly interested in history, as though he was rediscovering his own country. Massachusetts itself was always interested in supporting its own historical society. The very first large library in Boston had been founded in 1591, and, like most of the local libraries, had excellent collections of historical material. In England, Horace Walpole was predicting that Boston would produce a historian as great as Thucydides.

Many of those who had sailed from Salem to the South Seas had collected books, as we have learned, and books were a quality of life in Salem—not only in Salem, but in all of New England. There were journeymen who had six hundred books, although they did not own a pair of boots. The great minister Edward Everett and the historian, William Hickling Prescott had magnificent books and Rufus Choate, who left Salem to settle in Boston, filled his house with books, they said, floor by floor.

A young woman later reminisced to James Fields about Hawthorne when he returned from college. "He was even then," she said, "a most noticeable person, never going into society and deeply engaged in reading everything he could lay his hands on. It was said in those days he had read every book in the Atheneum Library in Salem." The woman remembered also that as a child she had sat on Hawthorne's knee and, resting her head on his shoulder, had heard the finest stories in the world, the ones he made up as he went along just to please a child.

Back in Salem, he was trying to please not only children but the growing artist that he was. "Be true!" he wrote later. "An artist must always be true to himself." Nothing swerved Hawthorne from his overwhelming dedication, his desire to experiment with all forms, his deep recognition that one must be true.

Hawthorne's own truth was all around him, in the landscape and story of his village. He would walk down the "long and lazy street to Witch Hill," which he described in "Alice Doane's Appeal," a story that may have been rescued from the burning mass of manuscript that made up *Seven Tales of My Native Land*. From Witch Hill he could look at Salem harbor, the gambrel roofs of the houses, the sharp glint of the water in the harbor, the fields and meadows.

He was alone and yet he was not lonely. "Grudge me not the day," he wrote, "that has been spent in seclusion, which yet was not solitude, since the great sea has been my companion, and the little seabirds my friends, and the wind has told me his secrets, and airy shapes have flitted around my hermitage. Such companionship works an effect upon a man's character, as if he had been admitted to the society of creatures that are not mortal."

Often he had less introspective adventures. With one of the Mannings he went to Connecticut on the coach: "We did not leave New Haven till last Saturday . . . and we were forced to halt for the night at Cheshire, a village about fifteen miles from New Haven. The next day being Sunday, we made a Sabbath day's journey of seventeen miles, and put up at Farmington. As we were wearied with rapid travelling, we found it impossible to attend divine service, which was (of course) very grievous to us both. In the evening, however, I went to a Bible class with a very polite and agreeable gentleman, whom I afterward discovered to be a strolling tailor of very questionable habits. . . . We are now at Deerfield (though I believe my letter is dated Greenfield) . . . with our faces northward; nor shall I marvel much if your Uncle Sam [their horse] pushes on to Canada, unless we should meet with two or three bad taverns in succession. . . .

"I meet with many marvellous adventures. At New Haven I observed a gentleman staring at me with great earnestness, after which he went into the bar-room, I suppose to inquire who I might be. Finally he came up to me and said that as I bore a striking resemblance to a family of Stanburys, he was induced to inquire if I was connected with them. I was sorry to be obliged to answer in the negative. At another place they took me for a lawyer in search of a place to settle, and strongly recommended their own village. Moreover, I heard some of the students at Yale College conjecturing that I was an Englishman, and to-day, as I was standing without my coat at the door of a tavern, a man came up to me, and asked me for some oats for his horse."

Another time he went to New Hampshire. "I walked to the Shaker village yesterday," he says, "and was shown over the establishment, and dined there with a squire and a doctor, also of the world's people. On my arrival, the first thing I saw was a jolly old Shaker carrying an immense decanter of their superb cider; and as soon as I told him my business, he turned out a tumblerful and gave it to me. It was as much as a common head could clearly carry. Our dining-room was well furnished, the dinner excellent, and the table attended by a middle-aged Shaker lady, good-looking and cheerful. . . . This establishment is immensely rich. Their land extends two or three miles along the road, and there are streets

of great houses painted yellow and tipt with red. . . . On
the whole, they lead a good and comfortable life, and, if it
were not for their ridiculous ceremonies, a man could not do
a wiser thing than to join them. Those whom I conversed
with were intelligent, and appeared happy. I spoke to them
about becoming a member of their society, but have come to
no decision on that point.

"We have had a pleasant journey enough. . . . I make in-
numerable acquaintances, and sit down on the doorsteps with
judges, generals, and all the potentates of the land, discours-
ing about the Salem murder, (that of Mr. White), the cow-
skinning of Isaac Hill, the price of hay, and the value of
horse-flesh. The country is very uneven, and your Uncle
Sam groans bitterly whenever we come to the foot of a low
hill; though this ought to make me groan rather than him, as
I have to get out and trudge every one of them."

He was getting to know New England history, and love
for it shone forth in such stories as "Endicott and the Red
Cross," "My Kinsman, Major Molineux," "The May-Pole
of Merry Mount," "The Gray Champion," "The Tales of
the Province House."

"Every individual," he wrote, "has a place in the world, and
is important to it in some respects, whether he chooses to be
so or not."

Hawthorne was finding his place in the world. And just as
James Joyce was to form precepts for himself by which he
would guide his writing, so did Nathaniel. In his notebooks
he said it was important for him to break off customs, "to
shake off spirits ill disposed, to meditate on youth, to do
nothing against one's genius."

But too often his spirits *were* "ill disposed." He was frequently depressed. Sometimes he complained, "We do not
even *live* at our house."

Legends were springing up that all the Hawthornes were

getting to be secluded and strange. Not only the mother, but the girls, too, were withdrawing from Salem society. Nathaniel was attracted to his solitude, but at the same time he knew that it was dangerous for him. Years later he wrote of those years, "I sat down by the wayside of life like a man under enchantment, and a shrubbery sprang up around me, and the bushes grew to be saplings, and the saplings became trees, until no exit appeared possible, through the entangling depths of my obscurity."

His own genius was his enchantment, and Hawthorne knew it. That room under the eaves "claims to be called a haunted chamber," he said, ". . . for thousands upon thousands of visions have appeared to me in it; and some few of them have become visible to the world. If ever I should have a biographer, he ought to make great mention of this chamber in my memoirs, because so much of my lonely youth was wasted here, and here my mind and character were formed; and here I have been glad and hopeful, and here I have been despondent. . . . And now I begin to understand why I was imprisoned so many years in this lonely chamber, and why I could never break through the viewless bolts and bars; for if I had sooner made my escape into the world, I should have grown hard and rough, and my heart might have become callous by rude encounters with the multitude. . . . But living in solitude till the fulness of time, I still kept the dew of my youth and the freshness of my heart."

Those Peabody Girls

"Oh, Sophia, you must get up and dress and come down! The Hawthornes are here and you never saw anything so splendid as he is—he is handsomer than Lord Byron."

That was the way Elizabeth Peabody remembered first describing Nathaniel Hawthorne to her sister Sophia, who was an invalid in bed upstairs. The Hawthornes and the Peabodys had known one another indirectly for many years since a common yard once had stretched between the two homes, and Elizabeth Hawthorne had once taken lessons from Mrs. Peabody, who had started a school for children.

Her oldest daughter, Elizabeth Peabody, thought the other Elizabeth a brilliant little girl, but the Peabodys had little to do with the boy. He was a broad-shouldered boy who seemed to like running about the yard more than studying. And as for Madame Hathorne, she was a recluse.

Elizabeth Peabody used to say that Madame Hathorne had properly withdrawn herself from the world, as it was good taste for a widow to do. But nonetheless, the Peabodys knew who the Hathornes were, because in those days everybody knew everybody else in town. As time went on, the Peabodys were to become better known.

Miss Elizabeth Peabody seemed to be omnipresent. She was also an omnivorous reader. She cut from magazine stories that particularly excited her—"The Gentle Boy," for example. Thinking that one of the talented Hawthorne girls had written the story, Elizabeth Peabody tracked down the Hawthornes.

"My brother's, you mean," said Miss Louisa.

"It *is* your brother, then; if your brother can write like that, he has no right to be idle."

"My brother never is idle," answered Miss Louisa quietly.

Indeed, Hawthorne was far from idle in those days.

The world, as he said, had called him forth, not too happily or too productively, but he was now far more conversant with the world of publishing. He had become the editor in 1836 of *The American Magazine of Useful and Entertaining Knowledge*, and for six months he read generally, storing up his own secret hoard of history and folklore, as well as popular and curious material that would appeal to the magazine's readers. Hawthorne received two hundred and fifty dollars for six months of steady work. His sister Elizabeth helped him with all the editing. She helped him again when he undertook *Peter Parley's Universal History* for the same publisher.

He had gone out into the world, and then suddenly the world greeted him. By the end of 1836, Nathaniel Haw-

thorne had a book in press, a book he was proud of, entitled
Twice-Told Tales. Hawthorne's old schoolmate, Horatio
Bridge, had guaranteed the publisher the cost of the volume.
Another schoolmate, Henry Wadsworth Longfellow, said in
a review, "Live ever, sweet book."

That desire came true. *Twice-Told Tales* lives today as
fresh as the "green leaves" that Longfellow discovered.
Hawthorne wrote to him in thanks:

"Whether or not the public would agree to the name
which you bestow on me, there are at least five persons who
think you the most sagacious critic on earth—viz. my mother
and my sisters, my old maiden aunt, and finally the sturdiest
believer of the whole five, my own self."

There were far more than five such critics. The Peabody
girls certainly augmented the list, and Sophia Peabody was
the strongest of champions.

Many marriages barely touch upon a writer's work. If the
writer is a man, one sometimes barely knows his wife exists.
But that is not true of Hawthorne's work or of his happiness;
he felt both were inextricably involved with his wife, Sophia.
Nathaniel Hawthorne's story is one of the great love stories
in American history.

One cannot say that Hawthorne had not been interested in
other women. There was even some talk of a duel. A girl
who interested Hawthorne at the time of his marriage was a
great tale-bearer, or so legend says, and according to it Hawthorne, not a hotheaded man by any means, challenged to a
duel one of his friends who had spoken poorly of her. Fortunately the duel came to nothing, but Hawthorne always felt
extremely guilty about the incident. When his old college
friend, Cilly, was later killed in a duel, Julian Hawthorne
said, "The affair was a terrible shock to my father, who felt
in a way responsible for his death," because he had set such a

poor example. Dueling was no way for Hawthorne to express himself, as he was soon to know. The printed word was the only weapon he could use effectively.

Sophia would be quieter, not so tempestuous as the girl for whom he had been willing to duel, and that was what Hawthorne wanted. The Peabody sisters had grown up in the Salem Hawthorne knew. Those old East India merchant houses were still noble and beautiful. Their magnificent rooms and high ceilings were as natural to them as the sunlight on the water.

Dr. Nathaniel Peabody, the father of the three girls, was a dentist in Salem. He had married Elizabeth Palmer, the granddaughter of General Palmer, one of the most famous generals of the Revolutionary War. In those days this was what was called "good stock." They had three daughters and three sons. Only one boy, however, lived to maturity.

As with many families of "good stock," however, finances were always a problem. Mrs. Peabody determined that the girls should have the best possible education. She used to say that she had never left her children with ignorant women who were sometimes rounded up as servants, but always with women of taste and gentility who liked to read Shakespeare.

Dr. Peabody, however, did not have the career his wife had envisioned for him. Instead, as many mothers did especially then, she dreamed about the glory of her own family, and her children said they sometimes thought they were from an exiled nobility.

Probably Hawthorne understood a little of this feeling, because he, too, had been brought up in a world in which the romance of yesterday was more important than the poverty of today.

Mrs. Peabody, to augment the family income, had started a school. It was in that school that Elizabeth Hawthorne was enrolled after Mrs. Peabody had convinced Elizabeth's recluse mother that it would benefit her daughter. Elizabeth Peabody was just four years old when she attended her mother's school, and was a companion of Ebe Hawthorne, who was six. Time, however, separated the Hawthornes and the Peabodys. Madame Hawthorne had taken her children up to Raymond, Maine, and the Peabody girls had left Salem to go to Lancaster, Massachusetts. It was only when they were all grown up that their paths were to cross again at Salem.

Now they were to come together again because of the daughter most like her mother—Elizabeth Peabody, who had a school of her own and who kept well in touch with all the literary undertakings of the time. One day she picked up a copy of the *New England Magazine* with one of Nathaniel's stories. She urged all the Hawthornes to visit them.

Despite Elizabeth's rushing up to Sophia, Sophia did not even bother to dress and come down the day Nathaniel first visited. Indeed, before her marriage that was the way Sophia often behaved. She was the family invalid. She suffered terrible headaches and, from the time she had had teething problems as a baby, she was in bed more frequently than she was out. She was interested in books, of course, and was a good painter, painting as she reclined on a couch, on a nearby easel.

Sophia found her sisters difficult to understand at times, although she loved them dearly. Elizabeth seemed hard-headed and arrogant, perhaps too aggressive. Mary, for her part, seemed to take too great a liking to the young and handsome Hawthorne and did a great deal of walking with him along the seashore.

Mary seemed to bring out great confidence in Hawthorne. He was now a steady visitor to their house, the Gumshawe House, impressions of which he later used in his writing. He told her of his great interest in literature for young people: after all, if you wrote for young people, he maintained, you were influencing the world where it should be influenced, where it was still fresh and bright.

The education of the young had become one of the major concerns of intellectual ferment all over the world. Suddenly, young people were being understood to have identities of their own instead of being thought of as miniature replicas of adults, living in an adult world, dressed in adult clothes, and having only abbreviated adult thoughts.

Nathaniel and Sophia Hawthorne's life together was to be involved in that ferment, because they were so much a part and parcel of their time. Hawthorne, when he decided to write books for young people, approached Mary, who in turn approached Horace Mann, who was to be one of the greatest educators America would ever see. Elizabeth was a friend of Bronson Alcott, also a great educator of the time but less successful, perhaps, in earning a living for his family, one of whom was Louisa May Alcott, who wrote *Little Women*.

Alcott and Elizabeth Peabody were two educators far in advance of their time. Alcott felt that one could approach education with the ease that one used in conversation. If a child was to be punished, Alcott said, why not let him whip the teacher's hand? In that way the child would feel such shame and guilt that he was not likely to create mischief again.

In the long walks with Mary by the seashore, Hawthorne heard of Alcott's theories and those of Horace Mann. But eventually he always put theory aside and went to see Sophia, because finally Sophia had risen from her bed and looked with favor upon Nathaniel Hawthorne.

Elizabeth always remembered their introduction—how,

when she said "My sister Sophia," Hawthorne had looked at her so intently that Elizabeth immediately thought: What if he should fall in love with her? Sophia was still an invalid in spirit and, when Hawthorne asked her to accompany him on his walk in the evening, she said, "I never go out in the evening, Mr. Hawthorne." But he said in a low, urgent tone, "I wish you would."

Sophia soon did go out for walks with Hawthorne. She also did a drawing for one of the stories in his book, and she told him a little of the trip to Cuba that had changed the pattern of her invalidism somewhat. Her family thought that such a trip might restore her health. Perhaps, too, separation from her mother made her feel less inadequate. In any case, as she was resting on deck, she saw a rope hanging down from the mast. She urged the captain to let her swing herself by the rope, so that she might learn to walk freely again that way. And indeed she did, much to the surprise of the captain.

Just as Nathaniel made Sophia eager and happy to accept the world again, so did Sophia effect the same transformation in Hawthorne. He began to say, "I wanted something to do with this material world," and he soon had "something to do" in the most material of all worlds when he was appointed weigher in the Boston Custom House. The men on the docks appreciated him, as they did later when he was a Custom House surveyor in Salem, but it was rough, grimy, exhausting work. Hawthorne had, however, an opportunity to make as much as $1,000 a year, and he knew this was money he could well use to make Sophia his wife.

His private letters give some indication of his life on the docks. He did not want to complain and said, "I do not mean to imply that I am unhappy or discontented, for this is not the case." But one senses from his letters that he was very tired. It was a good tiredness, however, a tiredness of physical exertion, and he felt in his heart that he was getting some kind of experience that would flow out "in truth and wisdom later on."

Long Wharf fortunately was cool on the hottest days of summer, for often a sudden shower would fall in the late afternoon. Hawthorne was able to note even then the beauties of nature and said, "There were clouds floating all about— great clouds and small, of all glorious and lovely hues . . . so glorious indeed and so lovely that I had a fantasy of heaven's being broken into fleecy fragments and dispersed through space."

In very cold weather the docks were freezing. He would go down into the cabins "of dirty little schooners and there, by red hot stoves, sit on a biscuit barrel and have a pot of tea." He reached the end of each day looking, he said, "like a chimney sweeper." "But the latter has the advantage over me, because after climbing up through the darksome flue of the chimney he emerges into the midst of the golden air and sings out his melodies far out over the heads of the whole tribe of weary earth-plodders. . . ."

"I detest all offices," he said later. Particularly he wanted nothing to do with politicians. Sometimes he rebelled against the dark dungeon of the Custom House. It was a "murder of a joyful day," he said, "to spend it in the dark dreariness of such a fussy old retreat."

He longed for the sunshine. When he was free again, he said, he would enjoy the world with the simplicity of a five-year-old. "Boston Common . . . living in Boston . . . blessed be God for this green tract," he said. But almost anything could make him happy: a sudden hawthorn bush in bloom (hawthorn naturally fascinated him); he called it "the footsteps of May traced upon the islands in the harbor."

As dirty as his job was, it gave him time to think. "I have

often felt that words may be a thick and darksome veil of mystery between the soul and the truth which it seeks," he said once. And he recorded many pictures in his mind that he would use later at "the loom of fiction."

Secretly engaged to Sophia, he wrote her some of the loveliest of love letters.

"Most beloved Amelia:

"I shall call you so sometimes in playfulness, and so may you; but it is not the name by which my soul recognizes you. It knows you as Sophia; but I doubt whether that is the inwardly and intensely dearest epithet either. I believe that 'Dove' is the true word after all; and it never can be used amiss, whether in sunniest gaiety or shadiest seriousness. And yet it is a sacred word and I should not love to have anybody hear me use it, nor know that God has baptised you so—the baptism being for yourself and me alone. By that name, I think, I shall greet you when we meet in Heaven. Other dear ones may call you 'daughter,' 'sister,' 'Sophia' but when, at your entrance into Heaven, or after you have been a little while there, you hear a voice say 'Dove!' then you will know that your kindred spirit has been admitted (perhaps for your sake) to the mansions of rest. That word will express his yearning for you—then to be forever satisfied; for we will melt into one another, and be close, close together then. The name was inspired; it came without our being aware that you were henceforth to be my Dove, now and through eternity. I do not remember how or when it alighted on you; the first I knew, it was in my heart to call you so.

"Goodnight now, my Dove. It is not yet nine o'clock; but I am somewhat aweary and prefer to muse about you till bedtime, rather than to write."

Hawthorne did not tell his mother or his sisters about his engagement. His sisters now were withdrawing a little from life, as did his mother.

The Peabody girls were more understanding. Hawthorne saw Elizabeth Peabody while he was in Boston. She had opened a new bookshop on West Street. It was going to be a new type of bookshop. People could meet there and discuss the exciting literary and cultural activities of the day. There would be magazines, many of them foreign. Many people were to call the shop "Miss Peabody's Foreign Bookshop."

Soon, with her administrative skill and determination, Elizabeth Peabody had moved her entire family to West Street in Boston. Her only remaining brother sold drugs there, and the strange bottles on the shelves beside the books, people remembered later, gave the shop a kind of magical quality.

Sophia did not work in the bookshop but was often upstairs working on her paintings. Now Hawthorne could see Sophia in Boston, but he tried to avoid the shop on Wednesdays, when it was "a babble of talkers," the babble coming mostly from Miss Margaret Fuller, that extraordinary woman who was out to educate all of New England.

Margaret Fuller had been a Boston prodigy. She had read Ovid at the age of eight, and she was one of the few women whom men accepted on her own terms, although she did not always accept men on theirs. Her influence on Boston society was tremendous, and most of that influence came from her "Conversations," as they were called, at Elizabeth Peabody's.

The Conversations started in 1839 and continued until 1844. Some people were sarcastic enough to say that the talking never stopped in all that time. Margaret talked about anything—Greek civilization, the place of women, Hindu mythology. She started each subject with a short introduction and then went on to ask questions or to offer criticism. One whole winter, for example, was devoted to the fine arts, and another to ethics. The women of Boston were eager to test their minds, and they appeared regularly for the Conversations, which began at eleven o'clock in the morning. Sometimes twenty-five or thirty women met there, of whom Thomas Wentworth Higginson said, "They were the most alert and active-minded women in Boston."

The truth was, however, that neither Sophia nor Nathaniel Hawthorne could ever be completely comfortable in the presence of Margaret Fuller. Their own love seemed far more interesting than Margaret's painful excursions into every form of culture.

Nonetheless, there was something for everybody in Elizabeth Peabody's bookshop. Elizabeth and Mary and Sophia's mother, Mrs. Peabody, found the older gentlemen extremely attractive. Mr. Alcott, who was writing now in the *Dial Magazine*, seemed to be a glorious prophet, foreseeing that almost anything was possible in this renaissance in New England, which was called "The New Day." There were the good Dr. Ezra Ripley and Theodore Parker and Dr. Channing, and the younger Mr. Emerson, who would come for a cup of tea but his soul was really communing with the stars.

There was Hawthorne for Sophia, Horace Mann for Mary, conversation for Elizabeth, and new ideas for everyone. For example, they asked, "Why not a Utopia? Shouldn't there be someplace where one can have ideal living circumstances, where man labors with both his hands and his mind, where he sows new ideas?"

Emerson said, "We were all a little mad that winter. Not a man of us but did not have a plan for some new Utopia in his pocket."

The country was feeling the impress of the Industrial Revolution. Man was becoming somewhat alienated from the soil and from the past that had made him and which he had made.

There was a desire to try to capture a sense of the rural happiness and contentment of times gone by, when there wasn't any care, or so people thought, except hoeing or haying or getting in the crops. And with that idea, a group who very frequently came to Miss Peabody's decided to found a community at Brook Farm in West Roxbury, Massachusetts. The idea struck a response in many people, and it appealed particularly to Nathaniel Hawthorne. True, he must have had some doubts about it, but he was tired of the work in the Custom House, tired of being covered with coal dust and never having enough time to write. Wouldn't it be better to go out, even if one were covered by the dust of the fields, and find a little time to write in the sweet rural attractiveness of West Roxbury?

Not everyone was quite so sure. After all, Mr. Emerson, who said before the formation of Brook Farm that "I think we ought to have bodily labor, each man, and that men must work by the sweat of the face," was arguing only a year later, "Why does every man have to be a farmer and go bungle with the hoe and harrow?" And it is true, as one looks back upon a great deal of the activity known as the Brook Farm experiment, that there was a good deal of bungling, not only with hoe and harrow but also with heart and hope.

Nathaniel Hawthorne had saved a little money from his hard-earned salary at the Custom House, and he invested in two shares in the joint stock at five hundred dollars a share. Perhaps this would be the opportunity he was seeking. Not only could he write, he could marry his Sophia. There were those who said, when Hawthorne joined the Brook Farm experiment, that he was more eager to write and to get married than to farm. He was never to deny it. He was not a reformer by nature. And he could sometimes see the humor in what these good people were trying to do.

The animals on the farm all had an identity, thought Hawthorne, and he said wickedly one day, "There is a most vicious animal in the yard. A transcendental heifer belonging to Margaret Fuller. She tries to rule every other animal and a guard has to be placed over her when the other animals come in and out." But it did not matter. He said if he could marry Sophia and write what he wanted to, he would become a milkmaid.

Brook Farm

Hawthorne whipped the snow from his coat and moved to the blazing hearth at Brook Farm. It was a wonderful old fireplace, and, as he sat there, the snow still melted from his hair and his face blazed with the fire. He could imagine that once a family of old Pilgrims might have sat here before this very fireplace, using a kettle like the one now heating the water for tea.

There shouldn't have been any snow at this time of year. When Hawthorne had started out from Boston on the twelfth of April, 1841, to drive to West Roxbury to join Brook Farm, the day had dawned springlike. But by noon there had been snow—it was, indeed, a tempest. The drive with Warren Burton, late of the Harvard Divinity School, had been a lonely one, and they were cold and not quite so excited as they had been before, when they had gone through occasional snow drifts and patches of woodland.

Only the houses showed any signs of life. There, smoke came from the chimneys with the smell of burning peat. They paid little attention to the people on the road. They had to do their best and make, as Hawthorne said, "good companionship with the storm."

When he arrived at Brook Farm, he said he was little better than an icicle. It was not a promising beginning to his stay in a Utopia.

Utopias were springing up all over the world. Robert Owen, who had founded a Utopia in New Lanark, in Scotland, had also established Harmony, on the Wabash River in Indiana. How wonderful it would be to have a cultivated group of people together, to have a true society worthy of the name, to have such people as Nathaniel Hawthorne joining in a great Experiment in Living.

Unfortunately, as Hawthorne discovered the very day after his arrival, his experiment in living began with a pitchfork. "We attacked a heap of manure," he said. His own words, written the following day to Sophia, reveal his first impressions. Sophia and Nathaniel were not yet married, but Hawthorne addressed her as if they were.

"Oak Hill, April 13th, 1841"
"Ownest Love,

"Here is thy poor husband in a polar Paradise! I know not how to interpret this aspect of Nature—whether it be of good or evil omen to our enterprise. But I reflect that the Plymouth pilgrims arrived in the midst of storm and stept ashore upon mountain snow-drifts; and nevertheless they prospered, and became a great people—and doubtless it will be the same with us. I laud my stars, however, that thou wilt not have thy first impressions of our future home from such a day as this. Thou wouldst shiver all thy life afterwards, and never realize that there could be bright skies, and green hills and meadows, and trees heavy with foliage, where now the whole scene is a great snow-bank, and the sky full of snow likewise. Through faith, I persist in believing that spring and summer will come in due season; but the unregenerated man shivers within me, and suggests a doubt whether I may not have wandered within the precincts of the Arctic circle, and chosen my heritage among everlasting snows. Dearest, provide thyself with a good stock of furs; and if thou canst obtain the skin of a polar bear, thou wilt find it a very suitable summer dress for this region. Thou must not hope ever to walk abroad, except upon snow-shoes, nor to find any warmth, save in thy husband's heart.

"Belovedest, I have not yet taken my first lesson in agriculture, as thou mayest well suppose—except that I went to see our cows foddered, yesterday afternoon. We have eight of our own; and the number is now increased by a transcendental heifer, belonging to Miss Margaret Fuller. She is very fractious, I believe, and apt to kick over the milk pail. Thou knowest best, whether, in these traits of character, she resembles her mistress. Thy husband intends to convert himself into a milkmaid, this evening; but I pray heaven that Mr. Ripley may be moved to assign him the kindliest cow in the herd—otherwise he will perform his duty with fear and trembling.

"Ownest wife, I like my brethren in affliction very well; and couldst thou see us sitting round our table, at meal-times, before the great kitchen-fire, thou wouldst call it a cheerful sight. Mrs. Barker is a most comfortable woman to behold; she looks as if her ample person were stuffed full of tenderness—indeed, as if she were all one great, kind heart. Wert thou but here, I should ask for nothing more—not even for sunshine and summer weather; for thou wouldst be both, to thy husband. And how is that cough of thine, my belovedest? Hast thou thought of me, in my perils and wanderings? Thou must not think how I longed for thee, when I crept into my cold bed last night,—my bosom remembered thee,— and refused to be comforted without thy kisses. I trust that thou dost muse upon me with hope and joy, not with repining. Think that I am gone before, to prepare a home for my Dove, and will return for her, all in good time.

"Thy husband has the best chamber in the house, I believe; and though not quite so good as the apartment I have left, it will do very well. I have hung up thy two pictures; and they give me a glimpse of summer and of thee. The vase I intended to have brought in my arms; but could not very conveniently do it yesterday; so that it still remains at Mrs. Hillard, together with my carpet. I shall bring them the next opportunity.

"Now farewell, for the present, most beloved. I have been writing this in my chamber; but the fire is getting low, and the house is old and cold; so that the warmth of my whole person has retreated to my heart, which burns with love for thee. I must run down to the kitchen or parlor hearth, where thy image shall sit beside me—yea be pressed to my breast. At bed-time, thou shalt have a few lines more. Now I think of it, dearest, wilt thou give Mrs. Ripley a copy of *Grandfather's Chair* and *Liberty Tree;* she wants them for some boys here. I have several copies of *Famous Old People.*

"April 14th, 10: A.M. Sweetest, I did not milk the cows last night, because Mr. Ripley was afraid to trust them to my hands, or me to their horns—I know not which. But this morning, I have done wonders. Before breakfast, I went out to the barn, and began to chop hay for the cattle; and with such 'righteous vehemence' (as Mr. Ripley says) did I labor, that, in the space of ten minutes, I broke the machine. Then I brought wood and replenished the fires; and finally sat down to breakfast and ate up a huge mound of buckwheat cakes. After breakfast, Mr. Ripley put a four-pronged instrument into my hands, which he gave me to understand was called a pitch-fork; and he and Mr. Farley being armed with similar weapons, we all three commenced a gallant attack upon a heap of manure. This affair being concluded, and thy husband having purified himself, he sits down to finish this letter to his most beloved wife. Dearest, I will never consent that thou come within a half a mile of me, after such an encounter as that of this morning. Pray Heaven that this letter retain none of the fragrance with which the writer was imbued. As for thy husband himself, he is peculiarly partial to the odor; but that whimsical little nose of thine might chance to quarrel with it.

"Belovedest, Miss Fuller's cow hooks the other cows, and has made herself ruler of the herd, and behaves in a very tyrannical manner. Sweetest, I know not when I shall see thee; but I trust it will not be longer than till the end of next week. I love thee! I love thee! I would thou wert with me; for then would my labor be joyful—and even now, it is not sorrowful. Dearest, I shall make an excellent husbandman. I feel the original Adam reviving within me.
"Miss Sophia A. Peabody,
   13 West-street,
      Boston."

Louisa, too, received full details of Brook Farm in a letter signed "Nath Hawthorne, Ploughman."

"Brook Farm, West Roxbury,
May 3rd, 1841"
"As the weather precludes all possibility of ploughing, hoeing, sowing, and other such operations, I bethink me that

you may have no objection to hear something of my where-about and whatabout. You are to know then, that I took up my abode here on the 12th ultimo, in the midst of a snow-storm, which kept us all idle for a day or two. At the first glimpse of fair weather, Mr. Ripley summoned us into the cow-yard, and introduced me to an instrument with four prongs, commonly called a dung-fork. With this tool, I have already assisted to load twenty or thirty carts of manure, and shall take part in loading nearly three hundred more. Besides, I have planted potatoes and pease, cut straw and hay for the cattle, and done various other mighty works. This very morning, I milked three cows; and I milk two or three every night and morning. The weather has been so unfavorable, that we have worked comparatively little in the fields; but, nevertheless, I have gained strength wonderfully—grown quite a giant, in fact—and can do a day's work without the slightest inconvenience. In short, I am transformed into a complete farmer.

"This is one of the most beautiful places I ever saw in my life, and as secluded as if it were a hundred miles from any city or village. There are woods, in which we can ramble all day, without meeting anybody, or scarcely seeing a house. Our house stands apart from the main road; so that we are not troubled even with passengers looking at us. Once in a while, we have a transcendental visitor, such as Mr. Alcott; but, generally, we pass whole days without seeing a single face, save those of the brethren. At this present time, our effective force consists of Mr. Ripley, Mr. Farley (a farmer from the far west), Rev. Warren Burton (author of various celebrated works), three young men and boys, who are under Mr. Ripley's care, and William Allen, his hired man, who has the chief direction of our agricultural labors. In the female part of the establishment there is Mrs. Ripley, and two women folk. The whole fraternity eat together; and such a delectable way of life has never been seen on earth, since the days of the early Christians. We get up at half-past four, breakfast at half-past six, dine at half-past twelve, and go to bed at nine.

"The thin frock, which you made for me, is considered a most splendid article; and I should not wonder if it were to become the summer uniform of the community. I have a thick frock, likewise; but it is rather deficient in grace, though extremely warm and comfortable. I wear a tremendous pair of cowhide boots, with soles two inches thick. Of course, when I come to see you, I shall wear my farmer's dress.

"We shall be very much occupied during most of this month, ploughing and planting; so that I doubt whether you will see me for two or three weeks. You have the portrait by this time, I suppose; so you can very well dispense with the original. When you write to me (which I beg you will do soon), direct your letter to West Roxbury, as there are two Post Offices in the town. I would write more; but William Allen is going to the village, and must have this letter; so good-bye.

Nath Hawthorne,
Ploughman."

"Miss Maria L. Hawthorne,
   Salem
     Massachusetts"

The days at Brook Farm were pretty much the same. If you were to make a fire in the kitchen, you had to rise at four o'clock. A horn was blown at a quarter to five, when all hands turned out to milk and to get started in the barns, taking care of the horses, pigs, and cattle. Breakfast was at half-past six. After breakfast everyone in the community was soon identified by his blue frock, the kind of agricultural smocks used in England centuries before. Everybody worked steadily until eleven-thirty, then the cows and pigs were fed, as, eventually, were the people. There was an hour or two of leisure and then work again, shoveling, hoeing, spading.

Most of the Farm's members seemed to enjoy the fact that they were so isolated from society, but Hawthorne, whom many were to say was the most isolated writer of his time, didn't like the isolation at all.

Nathaniel Hawthorne was greatly misinterpreted by many of his contemporaries. His natural shyness and his ability to stand apart, casting a professional eye on what was going on, were considered a kind of alienation from society. The truth was, he was more in the stream of living than many of those who flung themselves with wild abandon into some of the headier activities of life.

By midsummer of that first fateful year there was enough of a group at Brook Farm to be organized into three divisions —those who worked in the fields, those who had mechanical ability, and those who had domestic ability. Great care was taken that each group consist of three persons, an uneven number, so that a decisive vote could be cast to settle disagreements.

Brook Farm had students, too, and it was one of the first examples of coeducation in the United States. The "sweetest simplicity" was very appealing. The young Curtis boys, George William Curtis and his brother James Burrill Curtis, came to prepare for college at the Brook Farm Institute of Education. Lloyd Fuller, fourteen years old, the brother of Margaret, came for the same purpose. Some said he was just as overbearing as his sister, despite the fact that he was a good deal younger.

The leaders of the Farm, Mr. and Mrs. George Ripley, were almost saints, it was said. Brook Farm had been principally Ripley's idea and his wife joined him wholeheartedly. Mrs. Ripley, despite all the hard work, wrote to her friends, "More of laughing than of weeping we have had for the last few weeks. For a busy, merry household we are at Brook Farm."

Some were a little harsh toward the experiment. Enthusiasm was one thing, said Elizabeth Peabody, but enthusiasm did not butter parsnips.

Nathaniel Hawthorne, too, became disenchanted. He was finding it impossible to find time to write. As a matter of fact, even his penmanship was turning to scribble. Chopping wood all morning so disturbed the muscles in his hands that it became almost impossible for him to form proper letters.

He caught cold, and his brain, he said, was in a thick fog. All kinds of minor disasters struck the colony. William Allen was stung by a wasp on the eyelid (there were wasps' nests in many of the rooms) and looked like a blind giant, said Hawthorne.

Nathaniel was learning to be patient. He had not been half so patient in the Custom House or at Salem, he said, and at Brook Farm, he was learning at last. But, alas, he was acquiring almost an antipathy to pen and ink. His soul obstinately refused to be poured out onto paper, he said. Just because the community bought four black pigs, his happiness was by no means complete.

He wrote in his notebooks steadily. One entry foreshadows a character in *The Blithedale Romance:*

"Octr 9th, Saturday.

"Still dismal weather. Our household, being composed in great measure of children and young people, is generally a cheerful one enough, even in gloomy weather. For a week past, we have been especially gladdened with a little seamstress from Boston, about seventeen years old, but of such a petite figure that, at first view, one would take her to be hardly in her teens. She is very vivacious and smart, laughing, singing, and talking, all the time—talking sensibly, but still taking the view of matters that a city girl naturally would. If she were larger than she is, and of less pleasing aspect, I think she might be intolerable; but being so small, and with a white skin, healthy as a wild flower, she is really very agreeable; and to look at her face is like being shone upon by a ray of the sun. She never walks, but bounds and dances along; and this motion, in her small person, does not give the idea of violence. It is like a bird, hopping from twig to twig, and chirping merrily all the time. Sometimes she is a little vulgar; but even that works well enough into her character, and accords with it. On continued observation and acquaintance, you discover that she is not a little girl, but really a little woman, with all the prerogatives and liabilities of a woman. This gives a new aspect to her character; while her girlish impression still continues, and is strangely combined with the sense that this frolicsome little maiden has the material for that sober character, a wife. She romps with the boys, runs races with them in the yard, and up and down the stairs, and is heard scolding laughingly at their rough play. She asks William Allen to put her 'on top of that horse'; whereupon he puts his large brown hands about her waist, and, swinging her to-and-fro, places her on horseback. By the bye, William threatened to rivet two horseshoes around her neck, for having clambered, with the other girls and boys, upon a load of hay; whereby the said load lost its balance, and slided off the cart. She strings the seed-berries of roses together, making a scarlet necklace of them, which she wears about her neck. She gathers everlasting flowers, to wear in her [hair?] or bonnet, arranging them with the skill of dressmaker. In the evening, she sits singing by the hour, together with the musical part of the establishment—often breaking into laughter, whereto she is incited by the tricks of the boys. The last thing you hear of her, she is tripping up stairs, to bed, talking lightsomely or singing; and you meet her in the morning, the very image of lightsome morn itself, smiling briskly at you, so that one takes her for a promise of cheerfulness through the day. Be it said, among all the rest, there is a perfect maiden modesty in her deportment; though I doubt whether the boys, in their rompings with her, do not feel that she has passed out of her childhood.

"This lightsome little maid has left us this morning; and the last thing I saw of her was her vivacious face, peeping through the curtain of the carryall, and nodding a brisk farewell to the family, who were shouting their adieus at the door. With her other merits, she is an excellent daughter, and, I believe, supports her mother by the labor of her hands. It would be difficult to conceive, beforehand, how much can be added to the enjoyment of a household by mere sunniness of temper and smartness of disposition; for her intellect is very ordinary, and she never says anything worth hearing, or even laughing at, in itself. But she herself is an expression, well worth studying."

Nathaniel could see the value of learning to milk a cow, but he could also see that he wasn't writing the books he wanted to write, and he was nowhere near to making a home for Sophia. They had hoped to live at Brook Farm together, perhaps in a house of their own. But, as time went on, it seemed unlikely that Hawthorne could bring her there, or even that Brook Farm could long hold Hawthorne.

When Sophia visited the colony she could see that he was dissatisfied. It occurred to Hawthorne that perhaps if he did not become a working member of the community but remained a boarder, he might be able to do some writing.

He made a trip to Salem, and when he returned in the fall

to Brook Farm, it was as a boarder. This arrangement was a little better. Years later, Ora Gannett Sedgwick recalled those days when she had been a teen-ager at Brook Farm:

"There was a comfortable sofa in the hall, under the stairs, on which Nathaniel Hawthorne, who then occupied the front room at the right, used to sit for hours at a time, with a book in his hand, not turning a leaf, but listening with sharp ears to the young people's talk, which he seemed to enjoy immensely, perhaps with the satisfaction of Burns's 'Chiel amang ye takin' notes.' It is, however, but just to Mr. Hawthorne to say that, whatever use he made in *Blithedale Romance* of the scenery and 'romantic atmosphere' of Brook Farm, he cannot be accused of violating the sanctities of the home and holding up to public observation exaggerated likenesses of his associates there. I spent some delightful hours with him the winter he died, when he assured me that Zenobia represented no one person there. . . .

"I do not recollect Hawthorne's talking much at the table. Indeed, he was a very taciturn man. One day, tired of seeing him sitting immovable on the sofa in the hall, as I was learning some verses to recite at the evening class for recitation formed by Charles A. Dana, I daringly took my book, pushed it into his hands, and said, 'Will you hear my poetry, Mr. Hawthorne?' He gave me a sidelong glance from his very shy eyes, took the book, and most kindly heard me. After that he was on the sofa every week to hear me recite.

"One evening he was alone in the hall, sitting on a chair at the farther end, when my roommate, Ellen Slade, and myself were going upstairs. She whispered to me, 'Let's throw the sofa pillows at Mr. Hawthorne.' Reaching over the banisters, we each took a cushion and threw it. Quick as a flash he put out his hand, seized a broom that was hanging near him, warded off our cushions, and threw them back with sure aim. As fast as we could throw them at him he returned them with effect, hitting us every time, while we could hit only the broom. He must have been very quick in his movements. Through it all not a word was spoken. We laughed and laughed, and his eyes shone and twinkled like stars. Wonderful eyes they were, and when anything witty was said I always looked quickly at Mr. Hawthorne; for his dark eyes lighted up as if flames were suddenly kindled behind them, and then the smile came down to his lips and over his grave face.

"My memories of Mr. Hawthorne are among the pleasantest of my Brook Farm recollections. His manners to children were charming and kind. I saw him one day walking, as was his custom, with his hands behind his back, head bent forward, the two little Bancrofts and other children following him with pleased faces, and stooping every now and then with broad smiles, after which they would rise and run on again behind him. Puzzled at these manoeuvres, I watched closely, and found that although he hardly moved a muscle except to walk, yet from time to time he dropped a penny, for which the children scrambled."

It was obvious, however, that Hawthorne and Sophia must make other plans for the future. Brook Farm was totally unsuitable, and that fall their wedding date was set.

Sophia decided that she wanted what every girl wants—a June wedding. Mrs. Peabody was still treating the Peabody girls as children. Sophia was actually thirty-three—certainly no child. It was not to be a June wedding, after all, but it was held on July 9, 1842, in Elizabeth Peabody's back parlor adjoining the bookshop.

When Sophia saw Hawthorne on her wedding day, her heart lifted despite the rain. He was indeed a "sun shining through a cloud," she said. And it seemed a good omen that when Mr. Clark, the minister, pronounced that they were married, the sun "shone directly into the parlor on West Street."

They spent their honeymoon in Concord. It was a good trip from Boston to the lovely tree-lined village that was to be their home. They had great luck. They had been able to rent the Manse, the old house of Ralph Waldo Emerson in which he had written *Nature*. Neither had seen it, but they were able to get it cheaply and it had its own furniture. It did not matter that the old house smelled of the past, that there was a stuffed owl on the mantelpiece that seemed to look down with disapproval at the newlyweds, or that the drafts were severe. They were happy.

The Magic of the Old Manse

 10

Nathaniel and Sophia could hardly contain their excitement as the horses slowly made their way from Boston to Concord. Sophia was no longer interested in the life of an invalid. She wrote, "I feel better, and not in the least tired. It seemed miraculous that I was so well." It did indeed seem a miracle that, simply by marrying, Sophia's life as an invalid ended. She was to have another life now, one that gave her infinite happiness with Nathaniel and their children.

That first day, as the horses took the route down the long road through Lexington, then farther, stopping for a moment between the magnificent trees on the Concord streets, the Hawthorne's finally reached North Bridge. There stood a house that already belonged to history and which today belongs not only to history but to literature.

It was the Old Manse, as Nathaniel Hawthorne called it, a manse being the traditional home of the ministers of New England. This had been a minister's house, and one minister's ghost, claimed Nathaniel, still walked its rooms. Though Hawthorne called it the Old Manse, others called it the Emerson House. From it, Ralph Waldo Emerson's grandmother had watched the embattled farmers fighting the Battle of Concord at the beginning of the Revolutionary War. You could see the battlefield from the dining-room window.

The house's windows were magnificent—the kind they used in the eighteenth century, tiny panes that of glass cut up as if they were so many playing cards. On those windows are recorded some of the happy days of the Hawthornes at the Old Manse. You can, if you look out one of those windows today, see the spider-web writing made by a diamond on glass:

"Nath. Hawthorne. This is his study, 1843,"
and then, "Sophia's, inscribed by my husband at sunset April 3rd, 1843, in the gold light. SAH.
Man's accidents are God's purposes,
Sophia A. Hawthorne, 1843."

The Old Manse seemed to be filled with the gold light of happiness that both Nathaniel and Sophia brought each other. In a small chamber, Una Hawthorne was born. She was named for the heroine in Hawthorne's favorite book, *The Faerie Queen*. There were those who thought it was far too fancy a name for any child, and George F. Hilliard wrote to Hawthorne, "As to the name of Una, I hardly know what to say. At first it struck me not quite agreeably, but on thinking more of it I like it better. The great objec-

tion to names of that class is that they are too imaginative
. . . if your little girl could pass her life in playing upon a
green lawn with a snow-white lamb with a blue ribbon
around its neck, all things would be in a 'concatenation accordingly.' Imagine Sophia saying, 'Una my love, I'm
ashamed to see you with so dirty a face' or 'Una my dear,
you should not sit down to dinner without your apron.'
Think of all this before you finally decide." The Hawthornes had already decided. It seems very appropriate that
Sophia and Nathaniel were able to find the reality of a dirty
face and the magic of a romantic name in one child. Nathaniel, however, sometimes called her Onion.

At the Manse, Hawthorne had his patch of garden. There
he would stand, often staring at it in wonderment for hours
on end, they said, until some "thought him daft." He planted
peas and potatoes and squashes. "The garden flourished like
Eden." But there were, of course, ferocious weeds that Hawthorne never conquered. The garden had been made for him
originally by Henry Thoreau, as his wedding gift. When the
Emersons had told Thoreau there were to be newcomers to
the Manse, instead of sending over a gift that could stale or
perish, he had given a gift that would continue to live, a garden.

In the Old Manse there was room enough for all the Hawthornes' desires. On the left of the entrance was a sitting
room, and in that room on a table by the window was the
music box Sophia so loved. Directly opposite was a parlor.
Parlors in New England of that day were rarely used, but
the Hawthornes used theirs. They turned it into a dining
room and thus made it less depressing. This was the room in
which Sophia often heard the ghost of the old minister who
had once lived in the house. The two rooms the Hawthornes
most loved were Sophia's studio, in which she painted, and
the upstairs study, which was Nathaniel's. On the walls of

this room hung many old pictures of clergymen. They looked, said Hawthorne, "strangely like bad angels," and arrogantly he placed them in the attic.

Concord began to call. The Emersons came the first week after the wedding, and soon the Alcotts and Henry Thoreau. One day came "Queen Margaret," as Sophia called her— Margaret Fuller, who would have liked to have had her sister part of the Hawthorne household and suggested that she board there. Nathaniel was quite shocked. He wrote to Margaret, "Had it been proposed to Adam and Eve to receive two angels into their paradise as boarders, I doubt whether they could have been altogether pleased to consent." He wanted the solitude that has always been precious to him, and, now that he shared it with Sophia, was even more precious.

The Manse, said Hawthorne, was the first home he had ever had. When he was comfortable in a home, Hawthorne worked well. Here, he began to write *Mosses from an Old Manse*. Here, too, he wrote many of what would be the second series of *Twice-Told Tales*, and here he edited the journal of his friend, Horatio Bridge, *Journal of an African Cruiser*.

In Hawthorne's day, a visit to the Concord battlefield was a pilgrimage made by many. Today, the field is an Historical Site of the National Parks program, and it is almost impossible to reach it at any time, as Hawthorne did, alone, because it is so popular with Americans from all over the country. He went there often and wrote of it at length:

"Come, we have pursued a somewhat devious track in our walk to the battle-ground. Here we are, at the point where the river was crossed by the old bridge, the possession of which was the immediate object of the contest. On the hither side grow two or three elms, throwing a wide circumference of shade, but which must have been planted at some period within the three-score years and ten that have passed since the battle day. On the farther shore, overhung by a clump of elder-bushes, we discern the stone abutment of the bridge. Looking down into the river, I once discovered some heavy fragments of the timbers, all green with half a century's growth of water-moss; for during that length of time the tramp of horses and human footsteps have ceased along this ancient highway. The stream has here about the breadth of twenty strokes of a swimmer's arm,—a space not too wide when the bullets were whistling across. Old people who dwell hereabouts will point out the very spots on the western bank where our countrymen fell down and died; and on this side of the river an obelisk of granite has grown up from the soil that was fertilized with British blood. The monument, not more than twenty feet in height, is such as it befitted the inhabitants of a village to erect in illustration of a matter of local interest rather than what was suitable to commemorate an epoch of national history. Still, by the fathers of the village this famous deed was done; and their descendants might rightfully claim the privilege of building a memorial.

"A humbler token of the fight, yet a more interesting one than the granite obelisk, may be seen close under the stone-wall which separates the battle-ground from the precincts of the parsonage. It is the grave—marked by a small, moss-grown fragment of stone at the head and another at the foot —the grave of two British soldiers who were slain in the skirmish, and have ever since slept peacefully where Zechariah Brown and Thomas Davis buried them. Soon was their warfare ended; a weary night march from Boston, a rattling volley of musketry across the river, and then these many years of rest. In the long procession of slain invaders who passed into eternity from the battle-fields of the revolution, these two nameless soldiers led the way.

"Lowell, the poet, as we were once standing over this grave, told me a tradition in reference to one of the inhabitants below. The story has something deeply impressive, though its circumstances cannot altogether be reconciled with probability. A youth in the service of the clergyman happened to be chopping wood, that April morning, at the back door of the Manse, and when the noise of battle rang from side to side of the bridge he hastened across the intervening field to see what might be going forward. It is rather strange, by the way, that this lad should have been so diligently at work when the whole population of town and country were startled out of their customary business by the advance of the British troops. Be that as it might, the tradition says that the lad now left his task and hurried to the battle-field with the axe still in his hand. The British had by this time retreated, the Americans were in pursuit; and the late scene of strife was thus deserted by both parties. Two soldiers lay on the ground—one was a corpse; but, as the young New Englander drew nigh, the other Briton raised himself painfully upon his hands and knees and gave a ghastly stare into his face. The boy—it must have been a nervous impulse, without purpose, without thought, and betokening a sensitive and impressible nature rather than a hardened one—the boy uplifted his axe and dealt the wounded soldier a fierce and fatal blow upon the head.

"I could wish that the grave might be opened; for I would fain know whether either of the skeleton soldiers has the mark of an axe in his skull. The story comes home to me like truth. Oftentimes, as an intellectual and moral exercise, I have sought to follow that poor youth through his subsequent career, and observe how his soul was tortured by the blood stain, contracted as it had been before the long custom of war had robbed human life of its sanctity, and while it still seemed murderous to slay a brother-man. This one circumstance has borne more fruit for me than all that history tells of the fight.

"Many strangers come in the summer time to view the battle-ground. For my own part, I have never found my imagination much excited by this or any other scene of historic celebrity; nor would the placid margin of the river have lost any of its charm for me had men never fought and died there. There is a wilder interest in the tract of land—perhaps a hundred yards in breadth—which extends between the battle-field and the northern face of our Old Manse, with its contiguous avenue and orchard. Here, in some unknown age, before the white man came, stood an Indian village, convenient to the river, whence its inhabitants must have drawn so large a part of their subsistence. The site is identified by the spear and arrowheads, the chisels, and other implements of war, labor, and the chase, which the plough turns up from the soil. You see a splinter of stone, half hidden beneath a sod; it looks like nothing worthy of note; but, if you have faith enough to pick it up, behold a relic! Thoreau, who has a strange faculty of finding what the Indians have left behind them, first set me on the search; and I afterwards enriched myself with some very perfect specimens, so rudely wrought that it seemed almost as if chance had fashioned them. Their great charm consists in this rudeness and in the individuality of each article, so different from the productions of civilized machinery, which shapes everything on one pattern. There is exquisite delight, too, in picking up for one's self an arrowhead that was dropped centuries ago and has never been handled since, and which we thus receive directly from the hand of the red hunter, who purposed to shoot it at his game or at an enemy. Such an incident builds up again the Indian village and its encircling forest, and recalls to life the painted chiefs and warriors, the squaws at their household toil, and the children sporting among the wigwams, while the little wind-rocked papoose swings from the branch of the tree. It can hardly be told whether it is a joy or a pain, after such a momentary vision, to gaze around in the broad daylight of reality and see stone fences, white houses, potato fields, and men doggedly hoeing in their shirtsleeves and homespun pantaloons. But this is nonsense. The Old Manse is better than a thousand wigwams."

Concord had then, as it does now, a great pride in the past. It is extraordinary that at this moment in history so many of the great writers of the nineteenth century were to make it their home. Of these, the writer Hawthorne saw most was Henry Thoreau.

Just as Salem, Hawthorne's birthplace, seemed to supply him with some secret mystery that helped him create his books, so did Concord, where Thoreau was born, supply him with all the mystery and excitement he needed. Occasionally he would roam away from Concord for a while down to Cape Cod, or up to the White Mountains in New Hampshire, or farther up to Maine; but it was primarily in Concord that Thoreau underwent the ordinary experiences he wrote of in such extraordinary fashion.

Others had known and walked by Walden Pond, but only Henry David Thoreau conceived of living there, thereby enriching his own life and, with the book he wrote, *Walden Pond*, enriching the entire world of literature.

Thoreau was called "the genius of Concord." He had been born there on July 12, 1817, more than a dozen years later than Hawthorne, who gave him the affection one might give to a younger brother. The two had many interests in common. Thoreau's father had been descended from a long line of sea captains and merchants, as was Hawthorne's. Thoreau's people had come from the Channel Island of Guernsey, off the coast of England. There was, too, the history of wealth in the past. Thoreau's grandfather had made a success as a merchant in Boston after having, as was the custom of the time, accumulated a small fortune in privateering. But, as was the case with Hawthorne's family, the wealth had dwindled until it was almost a story half remembered, told to children.

Thoreau was nearly penniless when he met Hawthorne, and although the Hawthornes had very little, the little they did have seemed wealth indeed to Thoreau.

Hawthorne and Thoreau were friends of the outdoors. Henry and his brother John had made a famous trip rowing and sailing down the Concord and Merrimac Rivers in a boat they called the *Musketaquid*. The brothers had built the boat with their own hands just two years after Thoreau had been graduated from college. Hawthorne was delighted to hear of this exciting trip, and in their long walks Thoreau brought it to life for Nathaniel, as he can still do for you today.

It is recorded in his *Journal*, *A Week on the Concord and Merrimac Rivers*. It is as memorable a book as *Walden Pond* and *Cape Cod* and Thoreau's other pieces of fugitive writings; but when it was published in 1849, Thoreau had to pay to have it printed and, in all, 215 copies were sold, 75 given away, and the rest put away in the attic.

Thoreau persuaded Hawthorne to buy the boat that he and his brother had built. Hawthorne changed its name to the *Pond Lily*, after the beautiful pond lilies floating at the edge of the Concord River below the Manse.

Hawthorne thought he knew something about boats. He rowed well, he felt, but watching Thoreau handle the *Pond Lily* he learned more than he had ever known before. A boat responded to Thoreau as though it were a beautifully trained horse. Thoreau told Hawthorne that all one had to do was to will a boat and it would go wherever one chose. Thoreau wrote later, "He is the best sailor who can steer within the fewest points of the wind and exact the motive power out of the greatest obstacles. Most begin to veer and tack as soon as the wind changes from aft, and as within the Tropics it does not blow from all points of the compass, there are some harbors which they can never reach."

Thoreau was never content to let his words rest. He might be speaking of what really made a sailor, but he was thinking of deeper things. What, for example, made a poet? And after discussing a sailor he would say, "The poet is no tender slip of fairy stock who acquires peculiar institutions and edicts for his defense, but the toughest son of earth and of heaven." He used to say to Hawthorne, "It is the worshippers of beauty, after all, who have done the real pioneer work of the world."

Thoreau was always welcome at the Manse. He particularly enjoyed the music box, and Sophia, with that remarkable kindness which was part of her character, lent it to him. He was overjoyed. But, as Hawthorne said, "Thoreau really had to be seen outdoors to be appreciated." They made many expeditions on the Concord River or simply took walks. Emerson joined them on some wonderful skating trips down the Concord, which Sophia described. She thought Hawthorne moved like a Greek god, while Thoreau simply danced on the ice, half wild. Emerson seemed too weary to stand up properly. But he was older than Thoreau and Hawthorne and bore the weight of the title, "The Sage of Concord."

Hawthorne most enjoyed the time he spent with Thoreau the last summer in The Manse. At that time Thoreau had built with his own hands his hermitage at Walden. Thoreau stayed there for two years and two months, living completely "on the labor of my hands only."

It was Emerson, however, who first brought Hawthorne to Walden Pond, and it was with Emerson that Hawthorne had walked twelve miles to a village to see a Shaker community there. When Thoreau and Hawthorne talked it was likely to be about Indians and the natural world around them. With Emerson, Hawthorne talked about books. The two men discussed Walter Savage Landor, Sir Walter Scott, Margaret Fuller, or William Ellery Channing. Eventually Emerson read some of Hawthorne's stories—"The Celestial Railroad" was one—and soon the sage of Concord was saying that there was a serene strength in the writing of the mystical, quiet Hawthorne.

For all his friends and his happiness at the Manse, Hawthorne was considered somewhat strange by the townspeople. They were used to a bit more conviviality. They rarely saw him, for example, at the magnificent cattle fair in the fall, the high point of social life in rural Concord. George William Curtis, who had known Hawthorne at Brook Farm, said that when Hawthorne was at The Manse people really considered him a phantom. "Look," they would say, "at the gate. It has never been fixed at the door to the Manse. It's already overgrown with grass."

The Hawthornes had so little money that few lights gleamed from their windows—one reason why the villagers, on their rare trips past The Manse, wondered whether anyone was there at all. There was a knocker on the door that, in the old pastor's day, had been used constantly by the villagers. But they were a little afraid of this mysterious man, and no one touched the knocker unless he knew him well.

At times when the villagers saw Hawthorne hoeing in the garden, as they themselves might, they thought there was an eerie quality about him, as though the corn or melon seed he was putting in the ground were different, as though he himself might be an apparition. In the summer the Old Manse was even more of a mystery, sitting in the shadows of the ancient ash trees, the ground covered with moss. It was during this period, that Emerson, seeing Hawthorne sitting quietly by himself in a gathering, once wrote, "Hawthorne rides well his horse of the night."

And yet, although Curtis says that in the three years Hawthorne lived in the Old Manse he probably wasn't seen by more than a dozen villagers, he was, curiously, a man to whom people turned in an emergency. One dark night such an emergency occurred.

One of the Concord farmers had a daughter who seemed unusually delicate for a farmer's daughter. Her temperament was so lovely that she was remembered for many years. Her name was Martha, and she wanted to be something more than a farmer's daughter. Fortunately, she was able to go away to a school not far from Concord, where she won many honors. But, typical of the time, it was said that she had "grown out of her class," that the school had taught her graces she was not likely to have acquired as a farmer's daughter and that she certainly would not need as a farmer's wife.

When she returned to Concord, she felt lost. She tried to find friends, but she was shy and not "of the intellectual group of Concord at all." The "intellectuals" did not expect that a farm girl could share their thoughts. If she had met someone like Margaret Fuller, perhaps the girl would have been encouraged to come out of herself. But she was so shy, so withdrawn, that she tried to start a school of her own. But the children liked gaiety, and Martha was not a gay girl. She grew sadder as time went on. Those who knew her muttered that she no longer knew how to milk a cow or churn butter or fry pork. Finally, one summer evening, she left her father's home—for the last time.

After a while her father, noticing how long Martha had been gone, began to worry. He and the neighbors went to the nearby woods, calling her name and crying out in the dark night. They sensed something terrible had happened. Then someone said, "The river!"

Hawthorne was known to be an accomplished boatman. Although the villagers thought him strange and aloof, they went to ask his help. They were surprised at how much he cared about helping anyone who needed it. The boats put out into the Concord, boat after boat drifting slowly down with the current. The flickering torches made weird reflections upon the water, throwing out strange lights that trembled and struck out into the night like fireflies. The grasses on the marshy banks hung dark and dank. Both banks swarmed with people—some, sensation-hunters, but most, earnest searchers, fearful of what the night would reveal. Finally, in the night dew, one of the groups came upon a heap of clothing—Martha's—abandoned before she ended her life and her unhappiness in the Concord River.

It was one of Concord's more famous tragedies, and Hawthorne never forgot it. In later years, when he wrote *The Blithedale Romance*, he remembered that evening; and when, in that book, the body of Zenobia is found, the reader can still feel some of the terror and darkness Hawthorne shared with the villagers of Concord, some of the pain and anguish, and some of the torchlight he tried to throw on the strange feelings of the human heart.

During their stay at the Old Manse, the Hawthornes were painfully poor. Now that he had a child, it was obvious to Nathaniel that he had to try to go into the world again to make money. Hawthorne still had influential friends, such as Horatio Bridge and Franklin Pierce. One day they paid him a visit at the Old Manse. Hawthorne was chopping wood in the shed when they arrived. Sophia later observed, "How his friends do love him! Mr. Bridge was perfectly wild with spirits. He danced and gesticulated and opened his round eyes like an owl. He kissed Una so vehemently that she drew back in majestic displeasure, for she was very fastidious about giving and receiving kisses."

That evening they talked about business. The perfect job for Nathaniel Hawthorne, Bridge and Pierce decided, was for him to become a surveyor at the Salem Custom House. This was a political appointment. Throughout his adult life Hawthorne was a Democrat but, when he was finally made Surveyor, he found that the appointment had little to do with his political affiliations but rather with the fact that he was Salem's man of letters.

He was appointed to the post on April 2, 1846, for a four-year term. For a while, Nathaniel Hawthorne commuted from Boston to Salem on weekends, because it was unwise to move Sophia at that time, for their son Julian was born in the summer of 1846.

In September, 1847, the Hawthornes moved to 14 Mall Street in Salem. After the Herbert Street homestead, the Hawthornes lived at 18 Chestnut Street, and then Mall Street. All the houses are still standing. They shared the Mall Street house with Nathaniel's mother and sisters. It had a high study and there Hawthorne could write his heart out. But would he? For Hawthorne was wretchedly unhappy. He told Longfellow, as they walked along the Charles River in Boston, that he might never write again. Tired, depressed, his life now revolved around the Salem Custom House.

The Custom House

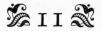 11

You can still walk up the steps of the Custom House in Salem and hear, in addition to the sounds of your own shoes on the stone steps, the distant sounds of all the sailors, sea captains, and business men of long ago who wore these steps smooth in the story of Salem.

These very stairs echo throughout the pages of Hawthorne's work, as they did indeed throughout his life. He climbed them over and over again many times a day in that period, from 1846 to 1849, in which he was a Surveyor. Those were the years of the last of Salem's great shipping days. In Hawthorne's first year, there were still some whalers out on long voyages. The ship *Elizabeth*, for example. The *Malay* had gone out earlier but had been wrecked in the Mozambique Channel. The *Emerald* had been wrecked at Madagascar and the *Sapphire* had come to an end in the West Indies.

The past was the past; the future of Salem was in doubt. In 1847, in the *Annals of Salem*, the Reverend Joseph Felt warned that whaling was at an end. "The prospect is that this perilous employment, recommended and hoped as to its increase, continuance and profit, will soon terminate in disappointment."

As he did throughout his life, Hawthorne took his work seriously. His was a dreary job, but he was glad to have it because it saved his family from near-destitution. It also gave him long periods of time just to think and to wonder. Many later critics of Hawthorne have observed that if he had not had to spend so many dry and dusty days as Surveyor, and later as a Consul, he might have written much more. True, he might have. But for the type of writing Hawthorne did—so deep and perceptive—there was need for long empty periods in which he could absorb his experience and replenish his emotion, so that he could expend them once again with glorious largesse. Gertrude Stein once said, "It is very hard to be an author. You must spend so much time doing nothing," and from time to time all writers must have a kind of hiatus in their lives in which they feed almost on the boredom of their daily experiences.

So each day Hawthorne walked up the steps of the Custom House and turned, as you may turn now, into the room to the left of the entrance. Here the National Park Service, which supervises the Custom House, has made it possible for you still to see the room in which he worked. It is an attractive room now, light and cheery, far cheerier and far lighter than it was in Hawthorne's day, when it was dusty with time and sawdust and, it seemed, perhaps even with some of Salem's own despair. You can push a button and hear a voice

tell you of Hawthorne's relationship to the Custom House
and then his own words echoing through the empty room:

". . . on the left hand as you enter the front door, is a
certain room or office, about fifteen feet square, and of a
lofty height; with two of its arched windows commanding a
view of the aforesaid dilapidated wharf, and the third looking across a narrow lane, and along a portion of Derby
Street. All three give glimpses of the shops of grocers, block-
makers, slop-sellers, and ship-chandlers; around the doors of
which are generally to be seen, laughing and gossiping, clus-
ters of old salts, and such other wharf-rats as haunt the Wap-
ping of a seaport. The room itself is cobwebbed, and dingy
with old paint; its floor is strewn with gray sand, in a fashion
that has elsewhere fallen into long disuse; and it is easy to
conclude, from the general slovenliness of the place, that this
is a sanctuary into which womankind, with her tools of
magic, the broom and mop, has very infrequent access. In the
way of furniture, there is a stove with a voluminous funnel;
an old pine desk, with a three-legged stool beside it; two or
three wooden-bottom chairs, exceedingly decrepit and in-
firm; and—not to forget the library—on some shelves, a
score or two of volumes of the Acts of Congress, and a bulky
Digest of the Revenue Laws. A tin pipe ascends through the
ceiling, and forms a medium of vocal communication with
other parts of the edifice. And here, some six months ago,—
pacing from corner to corner, or lounging on the long-
legged stool, with his elbow on the desk, and his eyes wandering up and down the columns of the morning newspaper
—you might have recognized, honored reader, the same individual who welcomed you into his cheery little study, where
the sunshine glimmered so pleasantly through the willow
branches, on the western side of the Old Manse. But now,
should you go thither to seek him, you would inquire in vain
for the Locofoco Surveyor. The besom of reform has swept

him out of office; and a worthier successor wears his dignity, and pockets his emoluments.

"This old town of Salem—my native place, though I have dwelt much away from it, both in boyhood and maturer years—possesses, or did possess, a hold on my affections, the force of which I have never realized during my seasons of actual residence here. Indeed, so far as its physical aspect is concerned, with its flat, unvaried surface, covered chiefly with wooden houses, few or none of which pretend to architectural beauty—its irregularity, which is neither picturesque nor quaint, but only tame—its long and lazy street lounging wearisomely through the whole extent of the peninsula, with Gallows Hill and New Guinea at one end, and a view of the almshouse at the other—such being the features of my native town, it would be quite as reasonable to form a sentimental attachment to a disarranged checker-board. And yet, though invariably happiest elsewhere, there is within me a feeling for old Salem, which, in lack of a better phrase, I must be content to call affection. The sentiment is probably assignable to the deep and aged roots which my family has struck into the soil. It is now nearly two centuries and a quarter since the original Briton, the earliest emigrant of my name, made his appearance in the wild and forest-bordered settlement, which has since become a city. And here his descendants have been born and died, and have mingled their earthly substance with the soil, until no small portion of it must necessarily be akin to the mortal frame wherewith, for a little while, I walk the streets. In part, therefore, the attachment which I speak of is the mere sensuous sympathy of dust for dust."

Today, opposite that dusty room is another chamber that leads into a small museum in which some of the history of Salem's great past is displayed. In Hawthorne's day this room, too, was dusty, filled with old surveying stamps and equipment, measuring tools and ancient scales. The old men hanging about the Custom House, were a sharp reminder to Hawthorne of the dustiness of the past, which, he felt, stood in the way of the present.

Whenever possible, Hawthorne tried to get out of the Custom House itself and onto crumbling Derby Wharf. He was there the first thing in the morning because he had heard that the men were paid according to the length of time they spent on the wharf itself. With his gentleness of spirit, he substituted for them until they themselves arrived, so as to make their day as long as possible. He often left his home in the center of Salem while it was still dark to get to the docks early.

Besides, he was never very happy away from the sea, he used to say, and here, with the sight of the circling gulls and the thin strip of sand skirting the edge of the dock near the street, some of the excitement of his early boyhood used to come back to him.

In those early hours he could look across the harbor to Marblehead; and in the evenings he watched the shadows behind Salem itself.

In bad weather he was always inside the Custom House, standing at an upright desk, gazing out at the wharf or into the past, or into his own imagination. He tried to steal whatever time he could for his writing because there was little enough room to work at home now. He had not had a proper study for nearly a year, using, instead, part of the children's nursery.

His wife had, however, made him a splendid writing gown, one in which he took enormous pride, a "Palm leaf, Moscow robe." Mrs. Hawthorne thought he looked quite regal in it. She did not like to see him tattered and torn, as he had been when they first arrived in Salem. Hawthorne did look very distinguished in the dressing gown, but he had a habit of wiping his pen upon its bright red lining. With great patience, Sophia made a tiny penwiper in the shape of a butterfly and sewed it over the blackest ink stain. He was delighted and amused.

Hawthorne often said that he never wrote successfully until the frost had fallen on the ground. In 1847 Mrs. Hawthorne made a notation, "My husband began retiring to his study on the first of November and writes every afternoon."

It was a productive period and a happy one. For once there was enough money and the two Hawthorne families lived together in relative ease. Hawthorne particularly enjoyed his children during this period, and some of his observations about Una appear in the child, Pearl, in *The Scarlet Letter*, although Pearl is hardly a true-to-life character but much more a fancy of the imagination. The Hawthornes kept a family journal, sometimes written by Sophia, sometimes by Nathaniel himself. Hawthorne's pleasure in his children is delightful. When they were away from him, which was seldom, he took care to include them in his letters.

"Salem, Surveyor's Office, June 19, 1848.

"Only Belovedest,—I received thy letter, and was as much refreshed by it as if it had been a draught of ice-water—a rather inapt comparison, by the way. Thou canst not imagine how lonely our house is. I wish, some time or other, thou wouldest let me take the two children and go away for a few days, and thou remain behind. Otherwise thou canst have no idea of what it is. And after all, there is a strange bliss in being made sensible of the happiness of my customary life by this blank interval.

"Tell my little daughter Una that her dolly, since her departure, has been blooming like a rose—such an intense bloom, indeed, that I rather suspected her of making free with a brandy-bottle. On taxing her with it, however, she showed no signs of guilt or confusion and I trust it was owing merely to the hot weather. The color has now subsided into quite a moderate tint, and she looks splendidly at a proper distance, though, on close inspection, her skin appears rather coarse. She has contracted an unfortunate habit of squinting, and her mouth, I am sorry to say, is somewhat askew. I shall take her to task on these matters, and hope to produce a reformation. Should I fail, thou must take her in hand. Give Una a kiss, and tell her I love her dearly.—Thine Ownest Husband."

"Salem, June 7, 1848.

"My dear little Una,—I have been very much pleased with the letters which you have sent me; and I am glad to find that you do not forget me, for I think of you a great deal. I bring home a great many beautiful flowers—roses and poppies and lilies and bluebells and pinks and many more besides—but it makes me feel sad to think that my little Una cannot see them. Your dolly wants to see you very much. She sits up in my study all day long, and has nobody to talk with. I try to make her as comfortable as I can, but she does not seem to be in very good spirits. She has been quite good, and has grown very pretty, since you went away. Aunt Louisa and Dora are going to make her a new gown and a new bonnet.

"I hope you are a good little girl, and are kind to your little brother, and Horace, and Georgie, and the baby. You must not trouble mamma, but must do all you can to help her.

"Dora wishes to see you very much. So do Grandmamma and Aunt Ebe and Aunt Louisa. Aunt Ebe and I went to walk together, a day or two ago, and the rain came and wet us a little.

"Do not you wish to come home and see me? I think we

shall be very happy when you come, for I am sure you will be a good little girl. Good-by.—Your Affectionate Father."

Hawthorne was halfway through writing a long short story when his mother fell dangerously ill. At the same time he heard with shock that he was to be dismissed from the Custom House because of political changes. His job had bored him, but it had meant a great deal to him. It had supported his family and given him a respectability in the town that he enjoyed.

He came home early the day he was finally dismissed. His wife was delighted to see him, but, as almost every man does sometime in his life, he told her he had left his head behind him. With the infinite love and understanding she felt for him, Sophia said, "Go then, you can write your book."

The book was *The Scarlet Letter*.

Through the long, hot summer his mother lay near death. The flies were unbearable, and Sophia Hawthorne spent most of her days with Mrs. Hathorne trying to keep away the flies and to make her as comfortable as possible. Hawthorne would sit in the nursery, or at the window, where he overlooked the yard and watched the children play. It seemed to him like a strange tapestry—a woman dying in one room and children, another generation, playing their games in another part of life.

He wrote faithfully at his book and also resorted to the old family journal—truly a family journal because it recorded the details of life around him. Writing is rarely divorced from living, and, as he wrote, he could hear Una crying for her mother, Julian, just three years, joining in the cries. He would watch both of them acting out the story of their grandmother's illness, one the doctor, the other the patient or the mother, until imagination had exhausted their play.

Finally Mrs. Hathorne died. Hawthorne was taken with

what his wife called a brain fever, but we know little about how long this depression lasted. The family began to discuss moving to the Berkshires, where the mountain air would bring back good health to them all.

In the meantime, there was very little money. Good friends came to their assistance, George Hillard among them. Others, the poet John Greenleaf Whittier, for example, made sure that magazines paid Hawthorne what was coming to him. His real solace came from his wife and children, but now, wretched and exhausted, Hawthorne was delighted to have an old friend visit him, James Fields, of the publishing firm of Ticknor and Fields.

James Fields carefully recorded that visit in the winter of 1849. He tells how he had found Hawthorne hovering near a stove in the chamber over the sitting room, which had been fitted out for his study. Hawthorne was still very despondent. Fields said, "Now is the time for you to publish, for I know that during those years in Salem you must have got something written and ready for the press."

"Nonsense," said Hawthorne. "What heart had I to write anything when my publishers have been so many years trying to sell a small edition of the *Twice-Told Tales?*" Then, and even more passionately, Hawthorne said, "Who would risk publishing a book for *me*, the most unpopular writer in America?"

"I would," said Fields with alacrity.

"What madness," Hawthorne said. "Your friendship for me gets the better of your judgment. No, no, I have no money to indemnify a publisher's losses on my account."

Fields began to be impatient; his train would soon be starting back to Boston. Yet he felt certain that Hawthorne had been writing during those years in Salem. Hawthorne still insisted he had written nothing. Fields looked around the room and his eyes fell on a bureau. Suddenly he was sure that what he was after lay in it. He said to Hawthorne, "There's something in there, I'm sure." Hawthorne simply shook his head. With a shrug, Fields started down the stairs. Hawthorne, startled by Fields's intuition, rushed to the bureau and thrust a roll of manuscript in his arms.

"How in heaven's name did you know that thing was there? As you have found me out, take what I have written, and tell me after you get home and have time to read it if it is good for anything. It is either very good or very bad—I don't know which."

The bundle of papers was what was to emerge as one of Hawthorne's two greatest novels, *The Scarlet Letter*. At that point, though, he had planned to make it just a long short story; it would be no more than two hundred pages in a new book to be called *Old Time Legends: Together With Sketches, Experimental and Ideal*. He felt that the somberness of the tale would be eased by the lightness of some of the other stories. A hunter loads his gun with a bullet and several buckshot, Hawthorne said, and many readers need several buckshot to grasp at instead of a single bullet.

Fields was able to convince Hawthorne that *The Scarlet Letter* should be a full-length book—and a great one—reflecting all the misery and unhappiness of the time in which it was set. Fields was right: *The Scarlet Letter* was to shine in the alphabet of American letters.

The Scarlet Letter

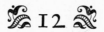 12

"Nathaniel Hawthorne writes romance."

"And what's romance? Usually, a nice little tale where you have everything As You Like It, where rain never wets your jacket and gnats never bite your nose and it's always daisy time. . . ."

"Hawthorne obviously isn't this kind of romanticist, though nobody has muddy boots in *The Scarlet Letter*. . . ."

"But there is more to it, *The Scarlet Letter* isn't a pleasant, pretty romance. It is a sort of parable, an earthly story with a hellish meaning."

The great writer D. H. Lawrence used this staccato method of shock alternating with insight when he wanted to discuss other writers. He felt this was the way to understand both art and the human heart.

The old Boston-to-Providence coach. Hawthorne made many trips on his uncles' coaches throughout New England, gathering impressions for his stories.

An early nineteenth-century print of a stable like the one Hawthorne frequented as a young boy when his uncles owned a coach line.

Contemporary cuts
of scenes that
Hawthorne loved.

A typical store of Hawthorne's
time, showing many of the
products brought in by the
sailing ships to Boston and Salem when Hawthorne worked
on the docks.

A nineteenth-century
"five dollar" school.

Portrait etching of Sophia
Peabody Hawthorne.

*Photograph courtesy of the Essex
Institute, Salem, Massachusetts*

Nathaniel Hawthorne's
portrait by George P. A.
Healey, painted for his
friend Franklin Pierce
in 1852.

*Photograph courtesy of the
Essex Institute, Salem,
Massachusetts*

Some famous Salem landmarks you may still see today. At left,
the Custom House, built in 1819. In the center, Hawkes House,
built in 1801. At right, Derby House, built in 1726.

Photograph by Eric H. Muller, courtesy of the National Park Service

Nathaniel Hawthorne's office
in the Custom House.

*Photograph courtesy of
Ralph Paterline*

The Salem Custom House,
where Hawthorne served as
Surveyor.

*Photograph by Eric H. Muller,
courtesy of the National Park
Service*

Looking out of the door
of the Custom House
toward Derby Wharf.

*Photograph courtesy of the
National Park Service*

The House of the Seven
Gables today. The
gables, said Hawthorne,
appeared to be a
"sisterhood of edifices,
breathing through the
spiracles of one great
chimney."

*Photograph courtesy of
Ralph Paterline*

Concord in 1840. *From an old print.*

Historical Old North Bridge, Concord, Massachusetts.
Photograph courtesy of the National Park Service

The "Sage of Concord," Ralph Waldo Emerson.

Louisa May Alcott,
author of *Little Women*,
a neighbor of
the Hawthornes.

Hawthorne's friend,
Henry David Thoreau,
in his traveling costume.
A sketch by his friend
D. Ricketson.

Herman Melville, the author of *Moby Dick*, one of Hawthorne's earliest admirers.

The Twitchell portrait, courtesy of The Berkshire Athenaeum, Pittsfield, Massachusetts

The Old Manse, to which Nathaniel Hawthorne took his bride Sophia.

Photograph courtesy of the National Park Service

The Wayside, in Concord, the last home of Nathaniel Hawthorne.

Hawthorne's grave in Sleepy Hollow Cemetery, Concord, Massachusetts.

Photograph courtesy of Carol Lewis and Shivaun Manley

Hawthorne was later to say in *The House of the Seven Gables* that the human heart is made from mud and marble. This conflict within the human heart is universal. Later psychology was to prove that Nathaniel Hawthorne was and continues to be one of the greatest writers who both used and attempted to understand the unconscious elements in man's life. Long before Freud he exposed these strange conflicts in everyone's life. Hawthorne tried to understand the hostility of the world, its cruelty and rejection of those who do not conform. He tried to understand the alienation of the human spirit.

The Scarlet Letter is a story of alienation. It tells of those who are alienated from one another, from society, and, worst of all, from their own selves. On the surface, *The Scarlet Letter* is a story of a woman, Hester, who has committed adultery; the minister of the community, with whom she committed the act; her husband, who neither loved nor understood her and who eventually seeks revenge; and the society outside that rejects Hester and her child, Pearl.

The scarlet letter was the letter "A," for adultery, but we can also think that that letter A stands for alienation, for the individual who will not come to terms with his own society or truly with his own self. But nothing is as it seems in *The Scarlet Letter*. Just as the letter A itself is a symbol, so many of the characters in the book are symbols, too. In one of his stories Hawthorne writes: "The heart, the heart. . . . Purify that inward sphere and the many shapes of evil that haunt the outward, and which now seem almost our only realities will turn to shadowy phantoms and vanish of their own accord." The idea that our conflicts are often projected onto the outside world was well understood by Hawthorne.

Actually, he seemed to anticipate many tenets of psychology. He says, for example, "Wherever there is heart and an intellect, the diseases of the physical frame are tinged with the peculiarities of these." This could be a definition of psychosomatic medicine today.

The deeper understanding of the pain and anguish and the essential aloneness of the human being was, however, Hawthorne's greatest contribution. In his time he had no way to approach this subject other than a crablike one. It had to be allegory.

The outline of his story had haunted him for a long time. Once, in the story "Endicott and the Red Cross," he wrote, "There was likewise a young woman with no mean share of beauty, whose doom it was to wear the letter A on the breast of her gown in the eyes of all the world and her own children. And even her own children knew what that initial signified. Sporting with her infamy, the lost and desperate creature had embroidered the fatal token in scarlet cloth, with golden thread and the nicer part of needlework; so that the capital A might have been thought to mean Admirable or anything other than Adulteress." The idea seemed to haunt him as he went through the old history books of colony law and he wrote again in his notebooks of the one who, when the Massachusetts Bay Colony had first been established, had been doomed to wear the letter A.

This idea persisted with Hawthorne. It had all the aspects of a good story but, in addition, he knew he could, more than in any of his other books, explore some of the deeper conflicts of the human heart. He could examine alienation and the isolation of the human heart in a variety of ways. Even the love between Hester Prynne and the Minister is an alienated love. It is doomed to failure before it begins. It is a love that goes against society, against the family, but, most importantly, against the possibilities for growth and satisfaction of both the main characters. Passion itself can alienate as well as attract. Hawthorne seemed to sense this.

Many later writers were to say that Hawthorne had a puritanical spirit, among them, as we have seen, D. H. Lawrence. It is true that no writer is completely aware of all the unconscious motivations of his writing. But it is obvious that Hawthorne knew and understood far better than many contemporary writers today that our lives are intermingled with the lives of all those around us. We must be responsible for our own actions and, alas, there are some actions for which we will be punished, at least made to feel uncomfortable, made to feel guilty. Some of these are just thoughts, some of them are actually moments that are temporarily satisfying but prove in retrospect not to be.

All the characters in *The Scarlet Letter* are separated one from another: the lovers, because their love was doomed from the beginning and they knew it; the husband and wife, because there never had been any effort at understanding; even the mother from the child. That wonderful child-character, Pearl, tries even as a small babe to understand why her mother must wear the A on her breast, and both mother and child suffer because of the mother's own inability to communicate with the child. There is no more beautiful section of *The Scarlet Letter* than the enchanting scene in which Pearl and her mother are near the seashore and the child gathers the seaweed at the beach and, imitating her mother, as children will, makes a green A out of grass and places it on her own chest.

Hawthorne showed great insight into children in his development of Pearl. "Children," he said, "have always a sympathy in the agitations of those connected with them; always, especially, a sense of any trouble or impending revolution, of whatever kind, in domestic circumstances."

Just as, when he was a small boy, he had been the observer, the spectator of all the minor domestic tragedies in his own home in addition to the one draining loss of his father, so finally he was able to observe and re-create a little of that anxiety in Pearl, the too-wild child, the fatherless child who tries to understand the adult world around her.

Eventually Hester Prynne makes her own adjustment to the world. She makes a better one than either her lover or her husband or even the society around her because she accepts her own guilt and, in accepting it, understands a little about herself. Her lover denies his guilt and so denies her, society, and himself.

These are all painful subjects and Hawthorne knew *The Scarlet Letter* was a painful book—a "hellish" book, he said. It is not quite so hellish to us today because we see that much of the pain of the various characters is of their own making. But if we read it more deeply we see it is a book that tells us more about our own time than many contemporary volumes.

A host of American writers following Hawthorne have been writing about the alienation of the human being in our own time. All the complexities of the technological world in which we live contributed to the fact that man was not making the right kind of adjustment either to himself or to society. At first this was just the author's province. The authors, as usual, tried to understand, tried to be, as Ezra Pound once called them, the antennae of the race. But today it is obvious that more than the writers feel the terrible alienation. The young people were some of the first to try to cope with it. Many people today feel that there is a revolution of the spirit going on in young people, that they are trying to find some proof of the essential validity of the spirit, but that they are going about finding it in many wrong ways. Hawthorne knew what the right map was; there was only one guide. It was the human heart, and in trying to understand one's own heart, one understood others as well. In all the pain and anguish of *The Scarlet Letter* the need for that understanding is paramount. Hawthorne knew that in everyone there was "the same cry of pain. What was it? The complaint of a human heart, sorrow-laden, perchance guilty, telling its secret, whether of guilt or sorrow, to the great heart of mankind; beseeching its sympathy or forgiveness—at every moment— in each accent—and never in vain!"

A Citizen of Somewhere Else

"I am a citizen," said Nathaniel Hawthorne, "of somewhere else."

With these words he said farewell to Salem. He was never to live there again. He left behind him a considerable amount of ill will. "My good townspeople will not much regret me," he said. They resented the fact that Hawthorne supposedly revealed a poor side of Salem in *The Scarlet Letter*. They said that the character of Judge Pyncheon was a thinly clad disguise for the man who had removed Hawthorne from the Custom House, and that some of Hawthorne's disdain for Salem's clinging to the past appeared in the "Custom House" introduction.

Hawthorne shrugged it all off. It is almost inevitable that a writer will be attacked by friends in places he has lived. It did not matter that Hawthorne had chosen a composite of Colonial Boston and Salem in which to set his story; but he had, of course, attached for almost no reason that extraordinary section called "The Custom House" to precede the novel and there he had captured the dust and motes in the eye of Salem's past.

The entire family breathed a sigh of relief as they settled down, in the little frame house that Hawthorne called "The Scarlet Letter," in Lenox, in western Massachusetts. The windows of the house looked down over Stockbridge Bowl, and at all times of the year, Monument Mountain shone above them.

The people of Lenox remembered Hawthorne for a long time. He looked, they said, like a banished lord. But he did not feel like that; he felt a discontent because he did not know what his next steps would be. He had felt exhausted during the past years. The illness of his mother and the concentration he had put into *The Scarlet Letter* had dulled the keenness of his perception. But now he began to see afresh, as he had in the observations of the earliest notebooks.

He took a great deal of pleasure in nature. He noticed everything: The red raspberries were just in season; the chestnut trees were snowy with blossom. He reflected upon the hen, looking for a place to deposit her egg; at the wasps and hornets and bees that came in the windows at which he worked.

He particularly liked the comments his children made, and he recorded them. The notebooks of the years at Lenox are filled with the children's delightful words and actions.

"When I grow up," he recorded Julian saying, "when I grow up I shall be two men." And Hawthorne pointed out that only a child could have that idea of strength. The boy would say in the fall, "Look, papa, here's a bunch of fire," or one of the children, drawing a cow, would say, "I'll kick this leg out a little more." How like a child to speak so of his drawing!

Sometimes Hawthorne would rest by the lake, his eyes shut, feeling the sunshine's warmth. With half-closed eyes, he could vaguely see the sparkling of light on the water. On other days it would be windy, and Monument Mountain looked, he wrote, like a headless sphinx.

"Lenox, February 12th, 1851.—A walk across the lake with Una. A heavy rain, some days ago, has melted a good deal of the snow on the intervening descent between our house and the lake; but many drifts, depths, and levels yet remain; and there is a frozen crust, sufficient to bear a man's weight, and very slippery. Adown the slopes there are tiny rivulets, which exist only for the winter. Bare, brown spaces of grass here and there, but still so infrequent as only to diversify the scene a little. In the woods, rocks emerging, and, where there is a slope immediately towards the lake, the snow is pretty much gone, and we see partridge-berries frozen, and outer shells of walnuts, and chestnut-burrs, heaped or scattered among the roots of the trees. The walnut-husks mark the place where the boys, after nutting, sat down to clear the walnuts of their outer shell. The various species of pine look exceedingly brown just now,—less beautiful than those trees which shed their leaves. An oak-tree, with almost all its brown foliage still rustling on it. We clamber down the bank, and step upon the frozen lake.

"The sunsets of winter are incomparably splendid, and when the ground is covered with snow, no brilliancy of tint expressible by words can come within an infinite distance of the effect. Our southern view at that time, with the clouds and atmospherical hues, is quite indescribable and unimaginable; and the various distances of the hills which lie between us and the remote dome of Taconic are brought out with an accuracy unattainable in summer. The transparency of the air at this season has the effect of a telescope in bringing objects apparently near, while it leaves the scene all its breadth. The sunset sky, amidst its splendor, has a softness and delicacy that impart themselves to a white marble world."

"February 18th.—A walk, yesterday afternoon, with the children; a bright, and rather cold day, breezy from the north and westward. There has been a good deal of soaking rain lately, and it has, in great measure, cleared hills and plains of snow, only it may be seen lying in spots, and on each side of stone-walls, in a pretty broad streak. The grass is brown and withered, and yet, scattered all amongst it, on close inspection, one finds a greenness—little shrubs that have kept green under all the severity of winter, and seem to need no change to fit them for midsummer. In the woods we see stones covered with moss that retains likewise a most lively green. Where the trees are dense, the snow still lies under them. On the sides of the mountains, some miles off, the black pines and the white snow among them together produce a gray effect. The little streams are the most interesting objects at this time; some that have an existence only at this season—Mississippis of the moment—yet glide and tumble along as if they were perennial. The familiar ones seem strange by their breadth and volume; their little waterfalls set off by glaciers on a small scale. The sun has by this time force enough to make sheltered nooks in the angles of woods, or on banks, warm and comfortable. The lake is still of adamantine substance, but all round the borders there is a watery margin, altogether strewed or covered with thin and broken ice, so that I could not venture on it with the children. A chickadee was calling in the woods yesterday—the only small bird I have taken note of yet; but crows have been cawing in the woods for a week past, though not in very great numbers."

He frequently walked with the children, finding berries, picking up Julian when he tumbled into a brook, sharing their delight in the first snow.

Sometimes they would walk with William Ellery Channing, the leader of the Unitarians in New England. They found the first wild strawberries with Channing. And Hawthorne took many walks and had many endless talks with a new friend.

The new friend was Herman Melville. "I met Melville the other day," Hawthorne wrote to his friend Horatio Bridge, "and like him so much I have asked him to spend a few days with me before leaving these parts." This was the beginning of an intense friendship, though the two men seemed quite unlike each other.

Melville was fifteen years younger than Hawthorne, not yet a writer of established ability—as Hawthorne would be soon with the publication of *The Scarlet Letter*—and a man of wild temperament and fierce outlook on the world. And yet Hawthorne had had many experiences with the type of sailor Melville was in those days when he was working on the story of his great white whale. By the time he was seventeen, Melville had been to sea. He had been all through the South Seas on a whaling ship; he had known the exotic islands of the South Pacific.

Perhaps the fact that he had seen so much of the world appealed to Hawthorne. But for his part, Melville seemed to like Hawthorne's view of the world—a view of the world being shaped and refined by his great imagination.

Melville was writing his book in Pittsfield, a short distance from the Hawthorne home, and he used to ride over with fair regularity to walk or talk with Hawthorne, whom he had admired for a long time. He had reviewed *Mosses from an Old Manse,* and when later he reviewed *The House of the Seven Gables,* he said something about Hawthorne that has been repeated in many books of contemporary American criticism. "He says no in thunder," wrote Melville, "but the devil himself cannot make him say yes. For all men who say yes lie and all men who say no, why, they are in a happy condition of judicious unencumbered travelers in Europe. They cross the frontiers into eternity with nothing but a carpetbag."

Melville said he felt that he and Hawthorne lived in "the all": they experienced as much of life as they possibly could.

Melville was a tortured man. He had the tornadoes of the Atlantic, he said, at the bottom of his soul, and he seemed a little like a shipwrecked sailor always tossed in the eddies of living. But in western Massachusetts he was on dry land at last.

Lenox at that time was a center of the arts. Many well-known persons had found their way there to make country homes. Fanny Kemble, the actress, often took the boy Julian Hawthorne riding horseback, pounding over the mountain paths. Dr. Oliver Wendell Holmes lived there in the summertime, and he said he had had the great honor of having the author of *The Scarlet Letter* hold his horse more than once.

Sometimes they all went up Monument Mountain together —Melville, Dr. Holmes, the publisher Fields, the lawyer and writer Henry Sedgwick, all of them caught in the showers that can cool the ardor of even the most enthusiastic climbers of western Massachusetts mountains.

Hawthorne was somewhat withdrawn. He disliked working in summertime. He felt it took him away so much from the beauty of the world outside, but he was, as Julian put it later, digesting the plan of *The House of the Seven Gables*.

At summer's end he began to work on it. He always noted houses well, and this story was to revolve around what he had noticed as a boy in some of the houses in Salem. In the meantime, he said he would love a soft, thick, Turkey carpet, crimson curtains for the windows so they would hide all the rectangles. He had almost a spiritual taste for beauty, Sophia insisted. They had been married more than eight years, but she never ceased to comment on his very special qualities.

If he could, Hawthorne would leave his study at noon instead of in the evening, the better to enjoy his children. They would read *David Copperfield* in the long winter evenings and then De Quincy. Once, on his desk, its brass scrubbed clean and a new cover upon it, Sophia wrote proudly, "Here Mr. Hawthorne wrote 'The House of the Seven Gables.' "

The House of the Seven Gables was written in five months, more quickly than most of Hawthorne's works and one of the most self-contained, but he himself thought it came to him quite slowly. On January 27, 1851, Sophia Hawthorne wrote in her diary.

" 'The House of the Seven Gables' was finished yesterday. Mr. Hawthorne read me the close, last evening. There is unspeakable grace and beauty in the conclusion, throwing back upon the sterner tragedy of the commencement an ethereal light, and a dear home-loveliness and satisfaction. How you will enjoy the book—its depth of wisdom, its high tone, the flowers of Paradise scattered over all the dark places, the sweet wallflower scent of Phoebe's character, the wonderful pathos and charm of old Uncle Venner. I only wish you could have heard the Poet sing his own song, as I did; but yet the book needs no adventitious aid—it makes its own music. . . ."

The House of the
Seven Gables

❧ 14 ❧

Come open the door of the House of the Seven Gables. As you step over its threshold, you can hear the clinking sound of sharp chimes, like those that used to tell Hepzibah and Phoebe somebody was waiting in the shop when they were in another part of the dark and gloomy house.

In this little shop now you can still find the kind of gingerbread men a hungry child used to try to bargain for when this was a small penny shop in the nineteenth century. You will not find, however, the other typical ingredients of such a penny shop. There are no needles or endless rolls of thread and yarn; there are no great bags of flour, no shelf of spices straight from the Salem ships home from their trips to the Orient. There are, of course, postcards and a copy or two of a book that has made this house famous: *The House of the Seven Gables*—a "romance," the author called it. Hawthorne stressed the fact that he did not call it a novel, but rather a "romance," made up a little out of the imagination, the mist of time, "the shadows of the picture" as the author used to call them.

It is perhaps Hawthorne's most appealing novel. He succeeded in what he wanted to do, to "connect the bygone times with the very present time." Even today, in this House of the Seven Gables in the town of Salem, you can feel what Hawthorne meant—despite the new developments and new buildings, the bygone time is conjured up for us, the sense of a glittering past.

Derby Wharf stretches out like a finger into the great Salem harbor, no longer beckoning ships from far away but almost calling aloud to the young people on hot summer days as they wander down its long point into the harbor. It is now part of the National Park Service of the United States, across the street from the National Historic Site of the Custom House. Just a short walk away, in a side street, almost buried in the Salem of yesterday, you come to Turner Street. Nearly at the foot of it (you are surprised by how much it embraces the water) is the House of the Seven Gables, now open to the public. Young people go through it in droves all summer long, thus supporting the settlement work of the organization that owns it. Hawthorne's enormous affection for young people would seem to make this a particularly appropriate memorial. He is not only still helping the young people of the community—the settlement teaches them all sorts of crafts—but he is also exciting them as he excited their parents, their parents' parents, and their great-grandparents before them as they walk through the door of literature.

You can open the pages of *The House of the Seven Gables* the way you open the front door of the house itself. You put your hand on the very first page of the volume, turn it over, and suddenly you will turn your heart over to Hawthorne's imagination and skill. The story captures you instantly, as the old house itself must have captured Hawthorne's imagination and as it can capture you if you return there today.

No one spot, of course, evokes a great book from any great writer. There are many who say that actually *The House of the Seven Gables* has little to do with the story Hawthorne wrote. Perhaps that is true. Hawthorne himself was very careful to point out it was made a little out of mist, but there is no doubt that the town of Salem and the surrounding land Hawthorne knew as a boy were always to influence his writings. Certainly, as one goes through the house and through the book's pages, the journeys back into time are similar—back into imagination, back into the curious interrelation of past and present that was Hawthorne's greatest skill.

So let us enter the house and the story. If we were to pass the little shop window that is the true beginning of *The House of the Seven Gables*, we would look into the past. First you can join Hepzibah as she plans her penny store in the House of the Seven Gables, which had been built on the land once belonging to one Matthew Maule. His well, they used to say, had been the most famous on the eastern coast. There, because of the fabulous water, Matthew Maule had built a hut. But in later years a Colonel Pyncheon lusted for the land and obtained it after Matthew's death—a curious death indeed, because Matthew Maule died on the scaffold as a criminal, for the horrible crime of witchcraft.

Legend has it that Colonel Pyncheon sat watching Maule on the scaffold, looking at him without a change on his countenance, and the dying man pointed to him and said God would give him blood to drink. *The House of the Seven Gables*, is a romance, of course, but, even as we hear those words, we hear a haunting evocation out of Hawthorne's own past. Those words were those of the curse that had been put upon his ancestor John Hathorne, the judge at the time of the witchcraft trials.

Hawthorne knew the House of the Seven Gables well. It had once belonged to the Turner family, then passed into the hands of Hawthorne's cousin, Susan Ingersoll. He visited it often as a small boy, making up stories even then out of the mist, as he was later to spin the romances that mark him one of our greatest writers. He used to go through the rooms checking their huge, strong beams. There are fourteen rooms in all, rooms hidden and buried and skirting the house, many of them with a gable window looking out to the sea or over the fields.

As a boy he would even go up on the roof and do as he had in many of the houses of Salem, lean against the gable and chimneys, and there, jammed safe from the winds coming in from the harbor, read the books he so loved, perhaps even old family letters he had found in the attic.

The past called to him; it seemed always trying to say something to him, and he listened the way others did not seem to be able to listen. Most boys, particularly at the age when the past began most to excite Hawthorne, are not interested in it. They are so concerned with the future and the world into which they must go, they do not quite understand why the past has anything to offer at all. Young girls, in contrast to young boys, do not feel this with quite the same alienation. They know they belong to both the past and the future the way all women must—raising one generation and explaining and hoping to continue the tradition of earlier generations. Perhaps the past haunted Hawthorne more because his father, who was part of it, had died so many years before; a little of its evocation was wondering what it would have been like if things had been different—if his father had lived, if the Hathorne family had taken its proper place in the community. In many of Hawthorne's stories you get this strange, haunting feeling of a family that has decayed a little, as the Hawthornes had decayed after the death of Hawthorne's own father.

So *The House of the Seven Gables* is the story of a family that was once great and is now less than great—indeed, it is poverty-stricken. The Pyncheons seem bound to the curse of a dying man, bound to their own curious foibles. Into this family and the old Pyncheon house comes Phoebe, a cousin —young, light as the sunshine itself,—for the Pyncheons, a line to the future as well as to the past. The Pyncheons had indeed been cursed, and the legend was that because of Maule's curious curse they had become so penniless that they were almost bond-servants to the Maules. In any case, Hepzibah and her poor brother Clifford seemed to be bond-servants to their own pain and to the past. The Maule children, on the other hand, it was said, had strange powers, mysterious attributes. And into that house to which Phoebe came, no Maule had stood for a long time. Or had he?

Was that quite true? One never knew about a Maule. Perhaps somewhere in the confines of the house the shadow or the ghost of a Maule still existed. The house looked as though it might contain many ghosts if one looked at it from the outside. Here is how Hawthorne himself described it:

"The street in which it upreared its venerable peaks has long ceased to be a fashionable quarter of the town; so that, though the old edifice was surrounded by habitations of modern date, they were mostly small, built entirely of wood, and typical of the most plodding uniformity of common life. Doubtless, however, the whole story of human existence may be latent in each of them, but with no picturesqueness, externally, that can attract the imagination of sympathy to seek it there. But as for the old structure of our story, its white-oak frame, and its boards, shingles, and crumbling plaster, and even the huge, clustered chimney in the midst, seemed to constitute only the least and meanest part of its reality. So much of mankind's varied experience had passed there—so much had been suffered, and something, too, enjoyed—that the very timbers were oozy, as with the moisture of a heart. It was itself like a great human heart, with a life of its own, and full of rich and sombre reminiscences.

"The deep projection of the second story gave the house such a meditative look, that you could not pass it without the idea that it had secrets to keep, and an eventful history to moralize upon. In front, just on the edge of the unpaved sidewalk, grew the Pyncheon Elm, which, in reference to such trees as one usually meets with, might well be termed gigantic. It had been planted by a great-grandson of the first Pyncheon, and, though now fourscore years of age, or perhaps nearer a hundred, was still in its strong and broad maturity, throwing its shadow from side to side of the street, overtopping the seven gables, and sweeping the whole black roof with its pendent foliage. It gave beauty to the old edifice, and seemed to make it a part of nature. The street having been widened about forty years ago, the front gable was now precisely on a line with it. On either side extended a ruinous wooden fence of open lattice-work, through which could be seen a grassy yard, and, especially in the angles of the building, an enormous fertility of burdocks, with leaves, it is hardly an exaggeration to say, two or three feet long. Behind the house there appeared to be a garden, which undoubtedly had once been extensive, but was now infringed upon by other enclosures, or shut in by habitations and out-buildings that stood on another street. It would be an omission, trifling, indeed, but unpardonable, were we to forget the green moss that had long since gathered over the projections of the windows, and on the slopes of the roof; nor must we fail to direct the reader's eye to a crop, not of weeds, but flower-shrubs, which were growing aloft in the air, not a great way from the chimney, in the nook between two of the gables. They were called Alice's Posies. The tradition was, that a certain Alice Pyncheon had flung up the seeds, in sport, and that the dust of the street and the decay of the roof gradually formed a kind of soil for them, out of which they grew, when Alice had long been in her grave. However the flowers might have come there, it was both sad and sweet to observe how Nature adopted to herself this desolate, decaying, gusty, rusty old house of the Pyncheon family; and how the ever-returning summer did her best to gladden it with tender beauty, and grew melancholy in the effort."

This house seems to take on a life of its own in Hawthorne's story. The story itself seems filled with hidden passages and strange gables and little diamond-cut windows looking out into the strange paths of human destiny. Harboring the spirits of Clifford, Hepzibah, and Phoebe, the house also has another member, the young photographic artist. Just who is he, this Mr. Holgrave? He is a wayfaring stranger, an intellectual who must come to terms with his heart, and, finally, emerges a Maule—but a new Maule, just as Phoebe is a new Pyncheon.

In moments of black despair, Phoebe brought light and happiness. Looking at Phoebe's charming face, Holgrave was never quite able to make love to the girl; no, he was too haunted by the past. "Shall we never, never get rid of the past?" he used to cry out. "It lies upon the present like a giant dead body." Phoebe did not quite understand him. Who could? What is this man who seems to be as haunted by the past as Hepzibah and Clifford are? But he is young and, as the saying goes, has everything to live for, and they are old and broken. Why should he, too, be so haunted?

Phoebe is somewhat annoyed by his comments. He seems

to hate the house, and he thinks that the green moss is too damp, that the rooms, the low-studded rooms, have too much grime and sordidness. He calls out that the house ought to be purified with fire. "Then why do you live in it?" Phoebe asks. "I dwell in it for a while that I may know the better how to hate it," and he tells her the story of Maule the wizard.

Actually, Holgrave's voice is partly Hawthorne's voice, a new voice pointing out the new ways New England must take because New England seemed at that point too much entrenched in the past. He says, "We shall live to see the day, I trust, when no man shall build his house for posterity. . . ." If each generation were allowed and expected to build its own house, he maintained, society would always reform itself.

The old and the new quarrel in this story. In it we can feel some of the tensions of Hawthorne's age in history. It was an age of great national advancement for the United States: railroads braced the nation, America's ships sailed the seas, and the telegraph linked whole sections of the world; inventions and inventors, books and writers, paintings and painters, seemed fruitful with a new destiny.

The characters in *The House of the Seven Gables*—Hepzibah, Clifford, Phoebe, the wicked judge, and Holgrave—are all determined by the greatest character of all—the house. To enter its door is to turn the lock upon adventure.

The world seemed ready for the publication of *The House of the Seven Gables*. "With great enjoyment," said Melville, "we spent almost an hour in every separate gable. This book is but a final chamber, abundantly but still deliciously furnished with precisely the sort of furniture best fitted to furnish it. There are rich hangings whereon are braided scenes from tragedies. There is old china with rare devices set about on the carved buffet. There are long and indolent lounges to throw yourself upon. There is an admirable sideboard, plentifully stored with good viands. There is a smell of old wine in the pantry, and finally, in one corner, there is a little black volume in gold clasps entitled 'Hawthorne, a Problem.' "

When Melville wrote that "Hawthorne, a Problem" haunted the House of the Seven Gables, he meant that even in one of Hawthorne's more gentle books, where, as Melville said, the sun comes in more and the genialities peep out more, Hawthorne had a haunting, almost tragic, understanding of some of the motivations of society.

Of the same piece of writing, Melville said, "We think that in no recorded minds has the intense feeling of the whole truth ever entered more deeply than into this man." Oliver Wendell Holmes was delighted with the book. The Yankee mind, he said, had previously grown only in pots of English earth, "but you have fairly raised yours as a seedling in the natural soil." Most critics thought *The House of the Seven Gables* a better book even than *The Scarlet Letter*, and Hawthorne himself admitted a certain pleasure in the later work that he had not found in the crueler outlines of *The Scarlet Letter*.

But all was not ideal. Suddenly Hawthorne was greatly disturbed by a letter that came to his attention, saying that a former resident of Salem had borne the name Pyncheon. There were also rumors in Salem that the wicked Judge Pyncheon was based on the Reverend Charles W. Upham, the man whom Hawthorne considered, in his wife's words, "the most satisfactory villain that ever was" and whom Hawthorne held responsible for his ouster from the Custom House.

Hawthorne often used names from Salem's past, taken from the gravestones in Salem's old cemeteries, but he never intended to have them identified with real persons. He always maintained that *The House of the Seven Gables* was a romance, and a romance is not based on real people. He wrote a conciliatory letter about his use of the Pyncheon name, which he said was quite accidental and undeliberate. And since he wanted to put out of his mind the pain of being challenged on any score, he was willing to insert a paragraph to the effect that he intended no reference to any individual. The statement never appeared, however, because his publisher was in London when a new printing went to press. Once again Hawthorne felt that Salem's ancient lore still seemed to be reaching out to oppress him.

Lenox

After the conclusion of *The House of the Seven Gables*, Hawthorne, like a good carpenter, rested from his building. The children remembered those months with the greatest pleasure. "He made them memorable to his children" said Julian later. "He'd fly kites with them, took them fishing and flower-gathering, and unsuccessfully tried to teach them swimming." Herman Melville would come in the evenings with his great dog, and the children would climb on the dog's back.

Everyone went nutting. Hawthorne was the best of all the nutters, standing on the ground, looking up into the trees. He would tell the children to close their eyes for a minute, and then there would be a sound of great rustling and scrambling, and there, soaring high, would be Hawthorne at the top of the tree, throwing down ripe nuts to the children below. Sometimes they would all go on an old-fashioned haymaking, in which the children were invited to neighboring farms. In the evening Melville would regale them with tales of his fighting with the savages in the Pacific.

For once Hawthorne began to work well in the summer, and he began his *Wonder Books*, one of the great treasures of childhood literature. His own children had heard all its stories—"The Snow Image," for example, which they vaguely remembered as one of their own experiences in the back yard in Salem. These stories in the *Wonder Books* were prefixed with little anecdotes or vignettes of life as it had occurred in the sweet hills of Lenox.

There was a new baby now. "She flourishes," said Hawthorne, writing to his sister Louisa, "and seems to be the brightest and strongest baby we have had." When Mrs. Hawthorne took her daughters for a visit to her mother, Julian was left alone with his father, and he remembered this time in later years as an uninterrupted succession of happy days. They took care of the rabbit together, and Hawthorne was never too busy to make many notes about it. "One finds himself," writes Hawthorne, "getting rather attached to the gentle little beast, especially when he shows confidence and makes himself at home." If letters did not come frequently from Sophia, Hawthorne would begin to fret. When they were expected and they did not arrive, he wrote, "It is nearly six o'clock by the clock, and they do not come. Surely they must, must, must be here tonight." And then with relief he writes in his notebook, "Within a quarter of an hour after writing the above, they come, all well. Thank God."

Despite the almost idyllic life in Lenox and Hawthorne's rich productivity, he began to be restless. He was never to find permanent rest anywhere again, said his son, and he soon became bored with any place in which he settled. He had left Salem behind, but with it he seemed to have left his roots and was only able to settle on the top surface of any spot to which he traveled.

Julian liked to think his father had the seafaring temperament of his ancestors, but Hawthorne seemed, instead, more like so many wandering writers, from Homer to D. H. Lawrence, who are always setting out on some kind of pilgrimage in part to uncover their own pasts. The truth is, of course, that Hawthorne found his own past most successfully when he was rooted in a place with which he was familiar, or which, as Lenox had, surrounded him with a serenity and beauty he seemed to need.

Hawthorne did think he might find this beauty and serenity in another house by the sea, but he could not find one. Instead, the family went to West Newton, to the home of his brother-in-law Horace Mann, who had gone to Washington when he was elected a representative to Congress. In West Newton the countryside was familiar to Hawthorne—it was within walking distance of what had been Brook Farm. And some of those memories came back to him now. They would be recorded in another book, *The Blithedale Romance*. West Newton, remembered Julian Hawthorne, was a dismal and unlovely little suburb in 1851. Julian, who was so aware of his father's feeling for his surroundings, said that Lenox drew forth *The House of the Seven Gables,* but West Newton was so ugly that a man had to write in self-defense.

The Blithedale Romance was modeled on Hawthorne's experiences at Brook Farm. Just as there were hidden Pyncheons ready to jump on him about *The House of the Seven Gables,* there were plenty of old supporters of the experimental utopian community who were annoyed by what they felt was his too accurate portrayal in *The Blithedale*

Romance. For in it is a wonderful character, Zenobia, a strange, tempestuous woman who many said was Hawthorne's interpretation of Margaret Fuller. Zenobia, however, was far more exciting than Margaret Fuller ever was. Some complained bitterly that it was Hawthorne's own insufficiency at the farm that colored his picture of the farm itself; but, once again, Hawthorne was not trying to portray anything accurately, let alone to capture on paper the extraordinary personality of Margaret Fuller. Friends were beginning to write to Hawthorne, Channing for one: "I know nothing of West Newton and do not wish to know any more," and he urged Hawthorne to find a more congenial spot. Why shouldn't he come back to Concord?—a place where he had been truly happy.

Channing teased him about where he could live. "What about the Gulf of Spezia, where Shelley had drowned? Or California? Or Venice?" Anything was better than the climate of western Massachusetts. "Absolutely the worst spot in the world," said Channing, "there are so many things against it, it would be useless to enumerate the first. Among others, day before yesterday, at six A.M., on the thermometer it was 10 degrees below nothing. That is enough."

Perhaps that was in part what attracted Hawthorne—remembering those cold winters of Maine. In any case, he decided that, yes, he would consider living in Concord again where they had been so happy in the Old Manse. Fortunately appropriately enough, just the right house came to their attention.

The Wayside

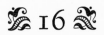 16

Henry David Thoreau surveyed the land for his friend. It was good land. There was a house on it standing fifteen feet from the old Boston Road. This had seemed appropriate to Hawthorne, who was still entwined, as all of Concord was, with the past. It had been on this very road that the British had marched and retreated. Across from the house, on the other side of the road, were eight acres of valuable land. "On the hither side," as Thoreau says, "this land extended a distance over the brow of the hill." It was not good for productive purposes, it couldn't be farmed, but was excellent for wandering, as Hawthorne was to discover for the rest of his life.

Thoreau, who knew all the local folklore of Concord as

well as he knew the palm of his hand, told Hawthorne that the house was famous. It had been inhabited a couple of generations before by a man who so longed for immortality that he believed he would never die. Hawthorne joked a little about this: "I believe, however, he is dead," he wrote. "At least I hope so; else he may probably appear and dispute my title to his residence."

But no one, including the resident who thought he would be immortal, disputed Nathaniel Hawthorne's right to the home where, except for his travels abroad, Hawthorne was to live for the rest of his life.

The house had belonged to the Alcotts. In their time, maintained Hawthorne, it was a mean-looking affair. It had no suggestiveness about it, no venerability. Bronson Alcott, who liked to manipulate his environment, had added a porch, a peak, and a piazza. But Alcott was more interested in the land than he was in the house. The land behind he built into terraces and arbors, and there was a summer house of rough tree stems and branches, "on a system of his own" muttered Hawthorne. Alcott was famous in the neighborhood for his own "systems." He had unusual ideas for raising and educating children; he even had "systems" for the laying out of land.

The Alcotts lived next door when Hawthorne moved to the house he was to call The Wayside. It had been called The Hillside by Alcott, but to Hawthorne The Wayside seemed more appropriate. Here he could sit by a true wayside, having emerged happily from that time when he had figuratively "sat down by the wayside like a man under enchantment."

Next to The Wayside was the Orchard House of Bronson Alcott. He lived in it for nearly thirty-five years, and it was in a structure that stood behind the one in which he held his summer School of Philosophy. "What is a philosopher?" someone once asked at one of these meetings, only to hear the wicked answer that a philosopher was a man attached to balloons that had to be held down by his family. His family, of course, was the family of *Little Women*. In one corner room of Orchard House, Louisa was to write *Little Women*. In its great attic Jo and Meg played; there was also a stage in the big barn on the hillside. Hawthorne later used Orchard House as the home for one of the leading characters in an unfinished novel called *Septimius Felton*. Louisa called this house Apple Slump.

In June, The Wayside seemed enchanted. Then the entire hillside, covered with locust trees, began to bloom, as did all the other trees coming into the full dress of summer. Throughout the years he lived there, Hawthorne planted more trees, more larkins and elms and oaks, pitch pines and firs and white birches, until this hill was marked with his own identity. Near the porch he planted a hawthorn tree.

Hawthorne liked to look over the low, wooded hills, across the meadows. "There is a peculiar quiet charm in these broad meadows and gentle eminences," he said. "They are better than mountains. . . . A few summer weeks among mountains, a lifetime among green meadows and placid slopes—such would be my choice." It was a calm and peaceful environment, and here he began to write his *Tanglewood Tales*. These simple tales for children were one of his favorite books. He had not abandoned the thought that one could place a great deal of one's self in books for young people, and that the young people, in turn, would understand and appreciate how much truth and vitality of spirit went into such stories.

But there was another kind of living going on for Hawthorne at this time. He who was the most unpolitical of men was once again to become embroiled in politics.

Franklin Pierce, Hawthorne's old friend at college, had

just become the Democratic candidate for the Presidency. Hawthorne realized almost instantly that Pierce would come to him for a campaign biography, as was usual at the time. Hawthorne said, "I was terribly reluctant to undertake this work and tried to persuade Pierce by letter and *viva voce* that I could not perform this as well as many others, but he thought differently."

It was a painful job. In the first place, there was little available material. In the second place, Hawthorne knew that many of his friends would turn against him because of his support of Pierce.

But Hawthorne was, above all, a true friend. His loyalty to his friends was strong throughout the years, and he felt, as did Pierce, that the world must move slowly and veer away from the civil war that was beginning to threaten the United States. Other writers, as Hawthorne said, "may have made larger claims for him and may have eulogized him much more highly. Any other could have bestowed a better effect of sincerity and reality in America. . . . Though the story is true, yet it took a romancer to do it," said Hawthorne. Yes, grumbled his critics, the work was one of fiction. Others immediately shouted that he was writing for money. Even Sophia's family turned bitterly against him.

Hawthorne was stubborn in his affection for Pierce. There were brighter men, he said, but Pierce had a directing mind. He knew how to administer, and that was what the country needed.

Sophia was always strongly behind Hawthorne. Her own affection for Pierce was considerable.

But outside opinions did not bother Hawthorne much in those days. What did it matter when one could walk among one's own woods? There was a great deal of walking now with the entire family. Sometimes, at least on the children's part, it would be to visit the Alcotts or the Emerson children —the Emersons had a particularly fine pony.

Sometimes Hawthorne would go over to see his nearest neighbor, Ephraim Bull, who had grew the first famous Concord grape, which was to revolutionize the grape industry in the United States.

One lovely October day in 1852, the entire family, except Rosebud, the new baby, who stayed with her nurse, mounted "their hill" and kept walking until they arrived at Peter's Path behind the Old Manse. Hawthorne had been happy in the Old Manse, but he thought he was happier now. As for Sophia, she said, "I am ten years happier in time and an uncounted degree happier in kind."

The family walked along the river with the water glistening like glass, and reached the area called Sleepy Hollow, which in a few years would be dedicated as a cemetery. There was a stately, broad path in Sleepy Hollow that Sophia and Nathaniel had long known. They called it the chariot road to a castle. It had been seven years since they had walked there, and the road now was surrounded by trees that had grown strongly. They sat on the ground for a long time, listening to the birds. Julian grew impatient, but he was fascinated by the colors of the trees and the rich crimson of the sumac. Both Julian and his mother were to remember that walk for the rest of their lives, because years later it was along that stately, broad path to the hill that Hawthorne's funeral procession was to pass.

But now there was no thought of unhappiness. There was superb coasting down all the hills. Hawthorne, Julian, and Una made one of the most famous snowballs in the neighborhood, so large that when it was put on the front lawn it did not melt until spring came.

Hawthorne knew, however, that things had changed. His

sister Louisa had died in a terrible fire on board the steamship *Henry Clay*. Sophia's mother was near death. Sophia was often unhappy now; it seemed that she was more and more separated from her sisters. The biography of Pierce had caused a great deal of resentment, and Horace Mann, her sister Mary's husband, was strongly against Hawthorne's political writing.

Sometimes, too, The Wayside seemed too decrepit for Sophia, and she would call it "a horrible old house." Although she added her paintings to the walls and Brussels carpets on the floors, nothing deterred the terrible flies that seemed to settle on everything. The water in the well, too, seemed dangerous.

Her brother-in-law, Horace Mann, had been nominated for the governorship of Massachusetts, but he chose to become the president of Antioch College instead. Antioch was to become one of the first colleges to educate women. Sophia was proud of her brother-in-law but she was protective, too, of her husband, for in those days he seemed to need even more protection than he had before.

When her mother died, Sophia threw herself into her love of her children, especially of the baby, Rose. Hawthorne was once more involved in the political scene. His closeness to Pierce, who, it now appeared, would be President, made him a political voice in Concord. Even Emerson, a political adversary, came to him for advice, as did R. H. Stoddard and even Herman Melville, who hoped he might become Consul in Honolulu.

Hawthorne knew after the election of Pierce that he could obtain some political appointment himself. He was eager for the post of Consul in Liverpool. Liverpool, because of its shipping, was of such major importance in those days that its Embassy was second only to the Embassy in London. Not only that, but it brought an extraordinary compensation for the day—up to $20,000, so it was said, although these were "fees" rather than a fixed salary.

On March 23, 1853, President Pierce nominated Nathaniel Hawthorne as Consul to Liverpool. The nomination went before the Senate and was confirmed. Charles Sumner, Hawthorne's friend in the Senate, wrote, " 'Good, good,' I exclaimed aloud on the Senate floor as your nomination was announced. 'Good, good,' I now write to you on its confirmation."

There were those, of course, who insisted that Hawthorne should not have taken such a post. But writing still paid him poorly, and he had a growing family to support. Sophia was discontented with The Wayside and would love to travel. Julian, now seven years old, was eager to see what the rest of the world was like. And Hawthorne himself was still seeking his roots. Had not the Hawthornes come from England; had not that been "our old home," as he called it?

Liverpool

❧ 17 ❧

Concord, complained Hawthorne, could be very warm and muggy in the summer, and on this hot July day, in his black clothes, he felt extremely uncomfortable. The children, too, were over excited at the prospect of their trip, but Sophia fortunately seemed to be holding up well. Sophia seemed as eager as did Nathaniel himself to see the England from which his family had once come and to which they were now returning.

The children had no thoughts about England. Their only thought was that they would spend several weeks aboard an old paddle-wheel steamer. Nothing could be more delightful to contemplate as, hot and sticky, they boarded the train that would take them to Boston. That evening they embarked on the *Niagara*. As Hawthorne stood on deck looking at Boston Harbor, his life seemed a sea lane leading to this moment. But if he turned his back on Boston and looked out to the infinite expanse of water stretched before him, he looked, he felt, to the future.

Captain Leitch of the steamer *Niagara* was everything a sea captain should be; in addition, he had bushy black whiskers and courteous careful manners. The *Niagara* was a small ship compared to ocean-going vessels of today—barely three hundred feet in length, a paddle-wheel steamer that, nevertheless, was the pride of its captain. There were some sailing ships still becalmed outside of Boston Harbor, and their crews gave a cheer as with the newfangled steam paddle-wheeled *Niagara* pulled seaward.

Hawthorne himself was a little depressed as he saw his land disappear from view, and he said to his son that "we should view with regret the disappearance of a land we might never see again." But he could not be sober about the sea for long. His son wrote later: "After we were fairly at sea, however, his gravity lightened and he gave himself up to the free enjoyment of the ocean he so dearly loved. His forefathers followed the sea, and he himself had scarcely ever lived out of sight of blue water."

This was the first extended voyage Hawthorne had ever made, and he seemed to benefit from it. "He never enjoyed such good health as when he was afloat," Julian said. "He was never seasick, spent all days on deck, and was never weary of watching the dance and rush of the waves and the changing hues and the lights and shadows of sea and sky."

He enjoyed watching the children, too—their delight in the voyage was extraordinary. The well victualed ships of those days always carried an amiable cow and some clucking hens aboard, and this touch of land brought to the children infinite pleasure.

On the eighteenth of July, the *Niagara* docked in the River Mersey. It was, as were so many English days that Hawthorne was to know, rainy. In those first days everything was exciting with the charm of the new. The first hotel was dark, as only the accumulated gray of Liverpool can be. But, as the ship had held in its bowels an amiable cow, the hotel held in its basement a large tank with three gigantic turtles that were a source of enormous pleasure to Hawthorne's children.

The family found its way eventually to Mrs. Blodgett's boarding house on Duke Street, an unusual hotel of the day that catered to the American captains who made voyages to Liverpool. Hawthorne felt immediately at home there. And when later, because of her health, Sophia had to take her daughters and go to Lisbon for a long period, Nathaniel and his son Julian lived with Mrs. Blodgett, happy in their vicarious following of the sea that they discovered in the old house. It was at Mrs. Blodgett's that Henry Bright once wrote a parody of "Hiawatha" based on Hawthorne's life in Liverpool. Hawthorne enjoyed it greatly.

SONG OF CONSUL HAWTHORNE

"Should you ask me, 'Who is Hawthorne?
Who this Hawthorne that you mention?'
I should answer, I should tell you,
'He's a Yankee, who has written
Many books you must have heard of';
For he wrote 'The Scarlet Letter'
And 'The House of Seven Gables,'
Wrote, too, 'Rappacini's Daughter,'
And a lot of other stories;—
Some are long, and some are shorter;
Some are good, and some are better.

And this Hawthorne is a Consul,
Sitting in a dismal office,—
Dark and dirty, dingy office,
Full of mates, and full of captains . . .
But you ask me, 'Where the dwelling,
Where the mansion, of this Hawthorne?'
And I answer, and I tell you,
' 'Tis a house in upper Duke Street,—
'Tis a red brick house in Duke Street.'
Should you ask me further, saying,
'Where this house in upper Duke Street?'
I should answer, I should tell you,
' 'Tis the house of Missis Todgers,—
House of good old widow Todgers,
Where the noble Yankee captains
Meet, and throng, and spend their evening,
Hairy all, and all dyspeptic,
All of them with nasal voices,
Speaking all through nasal organs,
All of them with pig tobacco,
All of them with Colt's revolvers.'
Should you ask me what they do there,—
What the manners and the customs
Of this house of widow Todgers,—
I should tell you that at Christmas
Mistletoe hangs in the parlors,
Mistletoe on hall and staircase,
Mistletoe in every chamber;
And the maids at widow Todgers',
Slyly laughing, softly stealing,
Whisper, 'Kiss me, Yankee Captain,—
Kiss or shilling, Yankee Captain!'
Slyly laughing, softly saying,

'Kiss from you too, Consul Hawthorne!
Kiss or shilling, Consul Hawthorne!' *
I should tell you how, at midnight
Of the last day in December,
Yankee Captain, Consul Hawthorne,
Open wide the mansion's front door,—
Door that opens into Duke Street,—
Wait to see the hoary Old Year
Pass into the frosty starlight,—
Wait to see the jocund New Year
Come with all its hopes and pleasures,
Come into the gas and firelight."

Henry Bright had met Hawthorne in Concord the year before. The son of a wealthy British shipowner, Bright had gone to Concord on a "literary pilgrimage." He was a great friend of Emerson's and he was as cheering to Hawthorne as his name. Hawthorne found it difficult to understand the British at first, and it was Bright who discussed and debated the English character with him.

Mr. Francis Bennoch was another of Hawthorne's close friends in England. One day, as he and Hawthorne were sitting in front of a fire, "Give me the poker, my dear Sir," said Bennoch, "and I'll give you a lesson." He seized the poker from Hawthorne's hand and gave the fire a sharp thrust. It broke into flames. "That's the way to get the warmth out of an English fire," he said, "and that's the way to get the warmth out of an English heart too. Treat us like that, my dear Sir, and you'll find us all good fellows."

It was with American sailors, however, that Hawthorne spent most of his time. He could not have been more at home with sailors if he had followed the sea himself. Now he was

---

* "A fib," wrote Nathaniel, when Bright gave him a copy of the poem.

to meet a motley crew. A dark, short, thickset sailor would come raging into the consulate, remove his hat, and say that he had been assaulted with a marlinspike. Julian Hawthorne, far more interested in blood and thunder than his father, inspected the wound with great pleasure. Julian was often in the office of the consulate. He sat on a chair that had been humped up with a couple of volumes of Congressional proceedings so that he was high enough to write elaborate letters to his relatives at home. They were far less fortunate than he was, he thought. All his life here in Liverpool seemed to be exciting. Everything about his father's job appealed to him.

It appealed much less to Hawthorne. He had hoped for a great deal of money as a result of the Liverpool appointment. Each ship that Hawthorne was responsible for as it came into the harbor entitled him to a certain payment, but not nearly so many ships came to the Mersey Pier as he had imagined. Still, the area abounded with ships: the *Great Britain* now lying right off Rock Ferry, where the Hawthornes had taken a home after they left Mrs. Blodgett's—she would be bound for Australia. Over there was a tall hulk of a ship of war, already dismantled and anchored in the river. Such ships were used as homes for old seamen. Up and down the river were many steamers going in all directions, and steamer tugs, and boats with dark red or tan-colored sails. The sails would be oiled so that they would resist the dampness of the river. Then there were the pleasure boats—the great yachts riding, said Hawthorne, "stately at their anchors."

The Mersey River itself had the color of a mud puddle, and the life of the waterfront always intrigued him. Beyond the waterfront were many of the city's poor sections—dark, lonely alleyways. There were beggars all over, bareheaded and barelegged in the deep of winter, and it seemed to Hawthorne they found every conceivable means of plying their trade.

The poor of Liverpool seemed very musical, and years later what was called the "Mersey Beat" emerged from the itinerant musicians who went through Liverpool's streets. Hawthorne described the musical ancestors of the Beatles: "Yesterday I saw a man standing bareheaded and barelegged in the mud and misty weather, playing on a fife, in hopes to get a circle of auditors. Nobody, however, seemed to take notice. Very often a whole band of musicians will strike up —passing a hat round after playing a tune or two. On board the ferry, until the coldest weather began, there were always some wretched musicians, with an old fiddle, an old clarinet, and an old verdigrised brass bugle, performing during the passage, and as the boat neared the shore, sending round one of their number to gather contributions in the hollow of the brass bugle. They were a very shabby set, and must have made a very scanty living at best. Sometimes it was a boy with an accordion, and his sister, a smart little girl, with a timbrel—which, being so shattered that she could not play on it, she used only to collect halfpence in. Ballad-singers, or rather chanters or croakers, are often to be met with in the streets, but hand-organ players are not more frequent than in our cities. . . .

"In the streets it is not unusual to find a band of half a dozen performers, who, without any provocation or reason whatever, sound their brazen instruments till the houses re-echo. Sometimes one passes a man who stands whistling a tune most unweariably, though I never saw anybody give him anything. The ballad-singers are the strangest, from the total lack of any music in their cracked voices. Sometimes you see a space cleared in the street, and a foreigner playing, while a girl—weatherbeaten, tanned, and wholly uncomely in face and shabby in attire—dances ballets. The common people look on, and never criticize or treat any of these poor devils unkindly or uncivilly; but I do not observe that they give them anything."

Hawthorne was always struck by how much life was spent in the open air. Those who could not afford shops simply set up their own markets in the street. The women sold combs, crockery was displayed, stacks of apples were precariously built on the pavement, herrings were laid out straight on boards, and coal was for sale everywhere.

Sometimes Hawthorne was saddened to see a child selling a personal article that seemed to be dear to him or her, and he was always pained at the speed with which the children moved to gather coal that fell from any of the carts passing by. It would be the only coal their homes would have.

He noticed that both the faces and the hands of the people were the same reddened color from the constant exposure to the cold air. And, as always, he was the observer of the most minute world. He frequently saw its shabby side because he moderated all cases of American sailors who were accused of any crime at sea. If an old sailor died, Hawthorne often went to his shoddy apartment to gather his pathetic collection of possessions. In such cases, Hawthorne had to attend the coroner's court, and he thought at one point that the diary of a coroner would be a wonderful idea for a book. It certainly would have, a large popular audience, he thought.

Throughout all his observations, Hawthorne realized that England was changing, even though England had yet to discover this herself. Progress was trampling over her aristocratic institutions, he said in his journals, and they were crumbling beneath it.

The great were seeking out Hawthorne now. Liverpool was second only to London in its importance as a consulship, and he was a person of importance in Liverpool. He had regular dinners with the mayors of British cities; bishops were there present in long tunics and black breeches and silk stockings; other civic dignitaries were there, and always there was the British food that Hawthorne grew to love—turtle soup and salmon, woodcock and oyster patties.

He dined on great ships that pulled into Liverpool—ships built by Donald McKay of Boston that were now making their name—and McKay's and Boston's name—known throughout the world, the way the ships of Salem had once been known when Hawthorne was a boy. At other times he would go below into the holds and hear the complaints of sailors. Always there were those for whom Hawthorne could do nothing. Hawthorne called them "exiles for liberty." And he was proud that the United States was now such a symbol of freedom that all came to his office—Hungarians and Poles, Cubans, Spanish-Americans, French sailors who showed their wounds, and Spaniards who brought little daughters.

In England, where American writers were being read and appreciated, Hawthorne was also respected as a writer. During his stay in Britain, more American books were being read than books from all of the Continent. At one point, England published twenty different editions of Walt Whitman, thirty-five by Edgar Allan Poe, sixty by Washington Irving, twenty by Henry David Thoreau, later sixty by Mark Twain, twenty-five by Emerson, and ninety—the largest of the lot by Hawthorne.

In the world of literature, England was truly Hawthorne's old home, and accordingly he went on literary pilgrimages to pay his respects to the homes and neighborhoods of writers of bygone days who had once influenced him when he was a boy reading on the rooftops.

The Literary Pilgrim

At times Hawthorne remembered the boy he had been, when he used to climb up to the roof in Salem, find a nook away from the wind, and read to his heart's delight. Now he permitted himself a dream to come true—he would follow the footprints of some of the great writers of the past who had so inspired his youth. Some of the happiest days of his stay in England and on the Continent were spent retracing the steps, seeking out the birthplaces, the homes, even the graves of these writers. Occasionally, of course, he would meet a living author, but even now, though he was a famous writer representative of his own country, he was too shy to speak. There was Tennyson, whom he saw wandering around in an art gallery. He described him vividly:

"Tennyson," he said, "is the most picturesque figure, without affectation, that I ever saw; of middle size, rather slouching, dressed entirely in black, and with nothing white about him except the collar of his shirt, which, methought, might have been whiter the day before. He had on a black wide-awake hat, with round crown and wide, irregular brim, beneath which came down his long black hair, looking terribly tangled; he had a long pointed beard, too, a little browner than the hair, and not so abundant as to encumber any of the expression of his face. His frock coat was buttoned up across the breast, though the afternoon was warm. His face was very dark, and not exactly a smooth face, but worn, and expressing great sensitiveness, though not at that moment the pain and sorrow that is seen in his bust. His eyes were black; but I know little of them, as they did not rest on me, nor on anything but the pictures. He seemed as if he did not see the crowd, nor think of them, but as if he defended himself from them by ignoring them altogether; nor did anybody but myself cast a glance at him."

Hawthorne was always delighted in pleasing Sophia, who accompanied him on this London trip, sometimes preferring to please her rather than himself. Rather than make the acquaintance of the great Lord Tennyson alone, he went to fetch her, but before they could meet the man whose poetry she and Nathaniel both so enjoyed, he had gone.

He went with his son Julian to the Shakespeare country. It was difficult to say who was the more excited—the boy who was reading for the first time the stirring pages of the great playwright or Nathaniel himself, who remembered his own excitement when he had first discovered Shakespeare.

He made his way to Newstead Abbey, the home of Lord Byron, and he took great pleasure in the library he saw there. He was delighted when the housekeeper took out a skull

Lord Byron had used regularly as a drinking goblet. It had a rim, it is true, of silver, but the rest was just naked bone. Hawthorne speculated that it would hold at least a quart of wine and that one would have to be very thirsty to use such a goblet. Hawthorne always enjoyed eccentricity. There had been so much of it in his own family, and as he looked at the skull he remembered a skull owned by one of his cousins that had been used as a spittoon. The New World could go the Old World one better even in the macabre.

Hawthorne was delighted when he went out into Byron's garden, which was similar to those he would fall in love with in Italy. There was a marble statue of Pan, for example, that had been brought back by the wicked Lord, the great-uncle of the poet. The country people, who were very afraid of it, said it was the Devil. There was a statue of Pandora; and at one tree Hawthorne stopped and wiped a tear from his eye, for this was the tree on which Byron had carved his name and that of his sister, Augusta. It was a birch tree, and the lines, he saw, had been deeply cut to last through the years.

He saw the place where Byron had buried his famous Newfoundland dog. But all the while Hawthorne seemed to feel there was a taint about the house, just as there had been "a taint in the Byron blood which makes those who inherit it wicked, mad and miserable," as Hawthorne said.

Nathaniel and Sophia took a trip to Scotland. After all, this was the home of Sir Walter Scott, who had brought so much joy to their New England childhood and who continued to be nightly family reading when Hawthorne returned to America. There in Scotland he was fascinated by the ruins, and he must have felt a sudden twinge in the reality of his name as he saw the hawthorn and the ivy gather around the desolate ruins. "I have not seen so much nor such thriving hawthorn anywhere else. . . . I saw in the outer court an old hawthorn tree to which a plant of ivy had married itself, and the ivy trunk and the hawthorn trunk were so absolutely incorporated, and in their close embrace you could not tell which was which."

Sophia and Nathaniel were disappointed in Abbotsford, the home of Sir Walter Scott. Hawthorne said, "Indeed it impressed me not as a real house intended for the home of human beings, a house to die in or to be born in, but as a plaything."

But Hawthorne found more interest in Scott's study. The servant taking the Hawthorne family around told Hawthorne he might sit in one of the chairs, adding, "You may catch some inspiration." The servant, of course, did not realize that Hawthorne was, as he said himself, a romance writer. " 'No, I shall never be inspired to write romances,' I answered, as such an idea had never occurred to me. I sat down, however."

Yet there was something disappointing about visiting these relics of a man who had meant so much to him. "I cannot but confess," he said, "a sentiment of remorse for having visited the dwelling place, as just before I visited the grave of the mighty minstrel and romancer with so cold a heart and in so critical a mood—*his* dwelling place and *his* grave, whom I had so admired and loved and who had done so much for my happiness when I was young."

For it pained Hawthorne to see the imperfections in writers who had influenced him. Perhaps it would be better to keep old heroes intact forever. He was much happier in the Lake District, where the homes of De Quincey and Wordsworth and Southey were far less elaborate and where the villages were still the villages of country people. Here in the Lake District Hawthorne was constantly walking, as Wordsworth, his sister Dorothy, Coleridge, De Quincey and Southey had before him.

The Hawthorne family went up the lonely winding roads,

roads barely more than paths; they looked down on glimpses of lakes great misty jewels. Sometimes, of course, it rained; then the whole family was uncomfortable. Una caught cold easily. There was a broken window in the hotel room, and Hawthorne had to put a copy of the *Times* against it to keep out the damp lake air.

There seemed nothing at all to do, Julian remembered. How familiar it sounds—just like any family on a vacation beset by damp and rainy weather. There were no newspapers, and Hawthorne complained, "Once you got away from the major cities in England no one seemed to be interested in what was happening in the world outside."

Although Hawthorne loved the country, he liked, too, what he called the great thoroughfares and centers of life—the anonymity and the excitement of the cities, but simultaneously he loved the solitude of the isolated areas of the world.

The Lake District reminded him of the White Mountains of New Hampshire, in which he had traveled during his young adulthood. But he almost preferred these mountains, these quiet hillocks of England. They looked, he said, "like crouching lions."

He noticed things minutely; for example, in front of one of the hotels in which he stayed, he examined two trees. "There are two trees," he wrote, "which we have hitherto taken to be yews but on examining them more closely, I find that they are pine trees and quite dead and dry, although they have the aspect of dark rich life. But this is caused by the verger of two great ivy vines which have twisted around them like gigantic snakes and clambering up and throttling the life out of them have put out branches and made clearance of sick green leaves so that at a little distance it is quite impossible not to take them for genuine trees. The trunks of the ivy vines must be more than a foot in circumference and one feels that they have stolen the life that belonged to the pines."

Sometimes he made remarks of a disparaging nature, or so it seemed to the British who were later to read his *English Notebooks*. One of the lakes, he said, he could easily carry away in a porringer. It was nothing more than a grass-bordered pool.

Throughout the *English Notebooks* you find an extraordinary wealth of detail and delight in the countryside of England and in its poets. He went to the house where Wordsworth died. Hawthorne was pleased when one of the old gardeners gave Julian a pine cone from Wordsworth's garden and that Sophia was able to get some leaves of laurel, ivy, and mignonette. He went to the little churchyard where he found Wordsworth's grave, and where eventually other Lake poets would rest. "The whole corner seems to be devoted to himself and his family and his friends," he said. As one reads his words one thinks of the Sleepy Hollow Cemetery in Concord where some of Hawthorne's family and friends rested in death, as in life, a little group apart. There, today we can make the same sort of pilgrimage Hawthorne in his day made to the Lake District.

Nathaniel reveled in the beauty of an English summer morning, everything moist and green and, as he said, "full of tender life." It is delightful travel writing, but Hawthorne, who was always well aware of what he was doing even when he was idly writing in his notebook, realized that he had not been truly able to capture the English Lake District. He said in disgust, "I am pretty well convinced that all attempts at describing scenery, especially mountain scenery, are sheer nonsense."

It had been a wonderful trip. Julian and his father had climbed to the enchanted castle; they had taken stagecoaches "more exciting than any train." They had eaten in strange places and had seen strange things.

Hawthorne continued to make brief escapes from the Consulate by traveling back and forth between Liverpool and the Lakes. But he found it a strain and said, "I am sick to death of my office—brutal captains and brutal sailors; continual complaints of mutual wrong, which I have no power to set right and which indeed seem to have no right on either side, calls of idleness, of ceremony for my travelling countrymen who seldom know what they are in search of at the commencement of their tour and have never attained any desirable end at the close of it; beggars, cheats, simpletons, unfortunates, so mixed up it is impossible to distinguish one from another and so, in self-defense, the Consul distrusts them all."

Many of the unfortunates he helped with money, others he helped as well as he could, but more and more he was conscious he was not writing. But still the literature of England was all around him. He went, for example, to Lichfield and Uttoxeter, towns closely associated with Dr. Samuel Johnson.

This particular literary pilgrimage seemed to bring back his childhood, as Hawthorne, now a grown man, walked among the scenes Johnson must have known—the Dr. Johnson he had met in Boswell's *Life of Johnson*. "Johnson had seemed," he said, "in his personal aspect to my mind's eye as the kindly figure of my own grandfather." "It is only a solitary child," he continued, describing his own childhood, "left much to such wild moods of culture as he chooses for himself while yet ignorant what culture means, standing on tiptoe to pull down books from those very lofty shelves, and then shutting himself up, as it were, between the leaves, going astray through the volumes at his own pleasure and comprehending rather by his sensibilities and affections than his intellect—that child is the only student that ever gets the sort of intimacy which I am now thinking of with a literary personage."

Hawthorne had such intimacy. "Dr. Johnson was great yeast," he said, "for a New Englander. He was so English, *so filled* with talk, so filled with memory." Hawthorne recorded that Johnson's father was a bookseller, and Hawthorne liked the idea of the literary wares laid out in the marketplace.

Hawthorne made a pilgrimage to old Boston, he traveled around Oxford, to the Burns country, and to a spot called Smithell's Hall. He wrote about it in his notebook.

"The entrance-hall opens right upon the quadrangular court; and is a large, low room, with a settle of carved old oak, and other old oaken furniture—a centre-table with periodicals and newspapers on it—some family pictures on the walls—and a large, bright coal-fire in the spacious grate. The fire is always kept up, throughout summer and winter, and it seemed to me an excellent plan, and rich with cheerful effects; insuring one comfortable place, and that the most central in the house, whatever may be the inclemency of the weather. It was a cloudy, moist, showery day, when I arrived; and this fire gave me the brightest and most hospitable smile, and took away my shivery feeling by its mere presence. . . ."

Smithell's Hall was to give him the idea for a novel he would work on spasmodically, but now, in January, 1855, the "Germ of a New Romance" seemed to ripen slowly in his mind. He was older and surer of himself, and he wrote to Longfellow, "Don't you think that the autumn may be the golden age both of the intellect and the imagination? Certainly *you* grow richer and deeper in every step of your advance in life. I should be glad to think that I, too, may improve—that, for instance, there may be something ruddier, warmer and more genial in my later fruitage."

It is true that Hawthorne was growing warmer and more genial, but he had little opportunity to write. Even the English Romance that he had mentioned was put aside.

Months went by, and it was decided that he would definitely resign his office, which he did, after four years, on August 31, 1857.

He described England vividly. Henry James was to say later that Hawthorne's writing about England was some of the most exciting he had ever accomplished. Certainly it is rich and fruitful. The *English Notebooks* document a period of time and history that is gone.

In the autumn the Hawthornes were ready to move again. They would go to the Continent but, as with all families, all were not ready to go at the same time, for the children got measles. It was not until the new year, January 5, 1858, that the Hawthornes left for Paris.

France and Italy

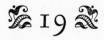 19

The cold was unbearable. Nathaniel Hawthorne always felt the cold intensely; but this strange European cold seemed to be more than he could bear. It had been miserably cold in England. And now, on the first holiday since Nathaniel Hawthorne had given up his Consulship, the family was equally cold in France.

The only thoroughly happy Hawthorne was Julian, who used to climb under the great eiderdown comforters and feel utterly relaxed. There were no such comforters in the New World—the inhabitants of the rugged New England coast were far too stern in temperament to have adopted such luxurious mounds of fluff and warmth.

Hawthorne used to look out on the Paris streets. It was as black as London, he said. There was a cold coat of sullen agony between each separate atom of the body.

Traffic was impossible. One could hardly get a carriage and, if one did, it was always going in the wrong direction. The little bookshops were dirty, but nevertheless the family used to go into them day after day, seeking refuge from the cold and miserable rain and mud.

And, like so many Americans traveling abroad, the Hawthornes acquired a traveling companion, that extraordinary woman, Miss Maria Mitchell, the astronomer who had recently discovered a new star. She fascinated the children. She seemed to have some intimate relationship with the stars themselves and, under her guidance, the young Hawthornes could point out carefully, with only an occasional mistake, all of the constellations.

Finally the Hawthornes had had enough of Paris. They must be on their way to their destination: Italy.

Italy was the goal of all thinking Bostonians in those days, and Florence was acquiring the reputation of being the Boston of Italy. There were Bostonians and Salemites and Concordites all over Italy's sunny land.

But where was the sun? It wasn't in Genoa, where the Hawthornes first stopped. They shivered through every palace and church, said Hawthorne. They traveled by carriage, and heard hair-raising stories of bandits who had attacked during such journeys. Hawthorne carried most of his money with him. He distrusted European banks and he hid his money in all sorts of places—in an old umbrella, for example. Julian thought it all was an adventure out of *The Faerie Queene*. Except for exhausted horses, however, nothing really happened to them. Once they did see two men framed against the evening sky at the top of the hill. Everyone held his breath—bandits, perhaps! But fortunately the men did not come down. The Hawthornes were safe. By the time they had reached the gates of Rome, sleet and rain were falling hard. When they arrived at the hotel, it seemed even wetter than the streets themselves, and Julian remembered that no one was warm for nearly a month.

"Sunny Italy," Hawthorne complained. "This is what is called sunny Italy and the reason why everybody in Massachusetts is leaving home—to see the sculpture and the artwork and the past of Italy and freeze."

Hawthorne sat huddled up near the fireplace; he had contracted a bad cold, and he looked like some great beast covered with rugs and greatcoats. He was extremely depressed. He did not know what he was looking for in Italy. Indeed, he wasn't quite sure that any of the Americans who seemed to be omnipresent from the tip of the Apennines to the boot of the Mediterranean knew. "All Rome," said Hawthorne, "lies like a dead and mostly decayed corpse, retaining here and there a trace of the noble shape it was."

When the sun finally did venture out, Hawthorne went to the fountains of the city. There, he acted as carefree as his son and skated on the ice, just to be able to say that he had done this in sunny Italy.

Toward spring, painfully, slowly, the Hawthornes had all thawed out. The third of March was Una's birthday (she was thirteen) and they celebrated it. They took a grand carriage and drove the whole family out on the Appian Way. It was the first warm day, and spring fever overtook all of them. Yet somehow or other Hawthorne distrusted the climate. There was too much dampness around, and people fell ill for no apparent reason. But he tried to forget such concerns on this wonderful holiday. He took Una to explore the ruins of one of the Gothic chapels near the roadway. They clambered through gaps in the wall. He showed her the ancient Roman pavement, and he thought of how different this highway was from the main street of Salem. The main street of Salem had known the primitive past of the Indian, but this knew a more distant past, a past crowded with people and with history. Even the smallest child, little Rose, enjoyed the outing, and her father took her even into tombs along the Appian Way.

On another day, the entire family went to the Coliseum. There the sun was bright and warm. Julian and his baby sister, Hawthorne was delighted to see, found "some beautiful flowers growing roundabout the Coliseum. And far up towards the top of the walls we saw tufts of yellow wallflowers and a great deal of green grass growing along the ridges between the arches." Julian was even happier searching for lizards, and Hawthorne, in his *Notebooks,* described his pleasure.

"Julian soon caught a large one with two tails; one, a sort of afterthought, or appendix, or corollary to the original tail, and growing out from it instead of from the body of the lizard. These reptiles are very abundant, and J—— has already brought home several, which make their escape and appear occasionally darting to and fro on the carpet. Since we have been here, J—— has taken up various pursuits in turn. First he volted himself to gathering snail-shells, of which there are many sorts; afterwards he had a fever for marbles, pieces of which he found on the banks of the Tiber, just on the edge of its muddy waters, and in the Palace of the Caesars, the Baths of Caracalla, and indeed wherever else his fancy led him; verde antique, rosso antico, porphyry, giallo antico, serpentine, sometimes fragments of bas-reliefs and mouldings, bits of mosaic, still firmly stuck together, on which the foot of a Caesar had perhaps once trodden; pieces of Roman glass, with the iridescence glowing on them; and all such things, of which the soil of Rome is full. It would not be difficult, from the spoil of his boyish rambles, to furnish what would be looked upon as a curious and valuable museum in America."

Hawthorne was too much a man of old Salem not to be constantly thinking of Massachusetts in relation to Italy. "At this very moment," he said, "I suppose the country within twenty miles of Boston may be two feet deep in snow and the streams solid with ice. But not here in Italy. Here we found open fields and lawns, moreover, all abloom with anemones, white and rose-colored and purple and golden, and far larger than could be found out of Italy except in hot-houses."

As the spring progressed, the family continued their jaunts, and made one to the Villa Borghese. There Hawthorne was struck by the fact that even the trees in this sunnier clime seemed to have a different calendar. "It seems to me that the trees do not put forth their leaves with nearly the same magical rapidity in this southern land, as they approach the summer, as they do in more northerly countries. In these latter, having a much shorter time to develop themselves, they feel the necessity of making the most of it."

When they were not on family picnics, Sophia and Nathaniel visited art galleries. Sophia was a determined gallery-visitor, and Hawthorne started to go too, reluctantly at first and then almost compulsively. Of all the plastic art forms, sculpture had always interested Hawthorne most. Salem had been a sculptured town, McIntyre having carved and whittled through the streets of the village. Hawthorne had been interested for a long time, too, in one of America's great early art forms—those magnificent carved ships' figureheads for the whalers and schooners. He had written a story of such a woodcarver in "Drowne's Wooden Image." But here in Italy it was stone that excited Hawthorne and the sculptors of his age.

At that time it was thought there was no stone in America that was sculptor's stone. One had to go to Italy to get it, and most of America's sculptors were making a sojourn in Italy of at least a year or two. "Marble," Hawthorne said bitterly, "to an American means nothing but white lawn stone."

The statues of fauns particularly caught his fancy. One day he saw a faun "copied from out of Praxiteles and another who seems to be dancing and exceedingly pleasant to look at. I like these strange, sweet, playful, rustic creatures linked so prettily, without monstrosity, to the lower drives. Their character has never, that I know of, been wrought out in literature, and something quite good, funny and philosophical, as well as poetic, might very likely be educed from them. The faun is a natural and delightful link betwixt human and brute life, with something of a divine character intermingled." As he wrote that in his *Notebooks,* he did not realize how powerfully the idea of the faun had caught hold of his imagination. So many things over the course of time stirred him, but he was not always aware of those that captured him as the faun did—a dancing, playful creature, playing and dancing with his imagination, which was to become the fabric of one of his greatest books.

Another day he went to the sculpture gallery and saw the original faun of Praxiteles. He said, "It was funny and wild at once. This race of fauns is the most delightful of all that antiquity imagined. It seems to me that a story with all sorts of fun and pathos in it might be contrived and the idea of their species having become intermingled with the human race, a family with the faun blood in them, having prolonged itself from the classic era until our days. The tail might have disappeared by dint of constant intermarriages with ordinary mortals, but the pretty hairy ears should occasionally appear in members of the family, and the moral instincts and intellectual characteristics of the faun might be most picturesquely brought out without detriment to the human interest of the story. Fancy this combination in the person of a young lady!"

The idea kept recurring to him all spring—to write a little romance about that faun—and he went regularly to the gallery, collecting notes.

When they weren't in the galleries, the Hawthornes were seeing friends. Many of them from New England were in Rome. There was the sculptor, W. W. Storey, who had been born in Salem and, living now in Rome, was carving, as so many exiles did, allegorical statues of America—of California, of Connecticut: symbolic marble carved of his own memory and dreams while he himself was in another country.

There was William Cullen Bryant, whom the Hawthornes had not seen since they had lived in the little red cottage in Lenox. He was a magnificent figure now, with a long white beard, "a brow almost entirely bald," said Hawthorne, "and what hair he has quite hoary. A forehead impending but not massive, dark bushy eyebrows and keen eyes without much softness in them."

They saw the Brownings. Hawthorne was a little shocked by the Brownings' son, still in dresses and with his hair long, who was hardly being brought up the way he was rearing his own son. And yet he was a sweet boy, looking remarkably like his mother, the invalid poetess Elizabeth Barrett Browning.

Mrs. Browning was such a pale, small person that Hawthorne said she seemed scarcely embodied at all. "Why, I do not see how Mr. Browning can suppose he has an earthly wife any more than an earthly child. Both are of the elfin race and will flit away from him some day when he least thinks of it."

There was Hawthorne's friend Hiram Powers, with whom he had endless discussions on the nature of art—how sculpture should be made, whether Raphael was a good painter. Even Michelangelo was capable of tricks, said Powers, and Hawthorne was rather shocked by the callousness with which Powers spoke of the greatest artists.

From Rome, the Hawthornes went to Florence. "This journey from Rome," said Hawthorne, "has been one of the brightest interludes of my life."

They found an extraordinary house, a castle, in which to live. It had a great tower, which was haunted, of course, and that appealed to Hawthorne because he always seemed to be living in a house some part of which was haunted. The tower looked over the valley of the Arno. If there had only been a little water for him to see from the tower, he would have been divinely happy. From the Hawthornes' tower, you could actually see the tower in which Galileo had made his famous astronomical experiment and another one across the gray groves of olives where Mrs. Browning had written "Aurora Lee."

There were ghosts in the tower, and also owls, and there was a strange, melancholy hooting, said Julian. Each night, the Hawthornes went to the tower and sat there looking at the stars and watching whatever thunderstorm might be coming over the hills. The house was called the Villa Montauto. Hawthorne called it Montebeni, and when he brought both the house and his idea of the marble faun together, they appeared in the book called *The Marble Faun or The Adventures of Monte Beni*.

The house had more than forty rooms, and Hawthorne, as he always did in old houses or castles, loved to explore them.

In a great subterranean basement, he found iron kettles and immense jars that must have been used for oil. There was a locked-up chapel out of which one could create any kind of mystery.

It was in this house that Hawthorne first started *The Marble Faun*. Castle or not, it was fit only for a summer home, and by the beginning of October the Hawthornes were back in Rome.

There, Hawthorne made plans. He would finish his romance in Rome and then go back to England, where he would get an English copyright. Then, surely, they would be back in their own United States by the summer of 1859.

But plans were suddenly changed. There were rules that one stuck to in the Rome of those days. One never, for example, went out into the night air after six o'clock. It was dangerous: malaria haunted the air.

One evening, Una Hawthorne and a friend stayed out beyond that time—the Roman ruins, her brother said, were too tempting. A few days later Una was down with malaria with its vicious chills and fever. She had what was called "the Roman fever." It began to undermine her strength seriously.

She grew weakened throughout the month, until she could not leave her bed. For four months she seemed to hover near death. A terrible winter set in, but Sophia Hawthorne nursed her daughter with enormous skill. For several days Una was unconscious. She had been muttering and crying out. Then, suddenly, she was quite still. Her mother, frightened at first, went to her bedside and put her hand on her head; for the first time, it was cool and moist—the crisis had passed. Sophia went to her husband and said simply, "She will live."

A good friend came to Hawthorne's aid in those days: General Pierce, no longer President of the United States, but now a world traveler. "I found all my early friend in him," said Hawthorne; "I recollect the first evening that Pierce came to our house and sat in the little parlor in the dusk listening to the story of Una's illness. 'Poor child, poor child,' he said." Pierce himself, as happened to so many people in those days, had lost both his children.

Hawthorne, who always, as he said, needed a serene outside life to be able to explore his inner life, could do no writing. As a matter of fact, the family had a hard time coming back to any sort of normalcy.

Relieved of the anxiety over the possible death of his daughter, Hawthorne for the first time enjoyed the extraordinary carnival spirit that at times overcame Rome. When he had first come to Rome, he took no interest in the carnivals, but now he studied them so carefully and enjoyed himself so much that Julian thought perhaps he was going to write a book about them. He did describe them in *The Marble Faun*. He noted everything as carnival time arrived—the masks of wire and pasteboard and silk, and some of the fantastic faces. Gently, he guided Una, his still-convalescing daughter, along the Corso. There he found rows of chairs set out on the sidewalk, baskets full of confetti, and bouquets of flowers radiant with the Roman sun. The carnival itself, Hawthorne felt, was strangely like a dream, and he enjoyed pelting people in cylindrical hats with handfuls of confetti. He had left his Consulate self behind, just as he had given up his black suits. But, as the days went on, he thought the merrymakers labored harder to be mirthful, and the sun stopped shining.

Carnival time moved on into spring. It was a Roman spring that Hawthorne particularly enjoyed. His spirits now were good—he was thinking of the family's return to the United States that summer. Again it was not to be because of various publishing problems that awaited him in England.

When the Hawthornes arrived in England, it became apparent the family finances were such that Nathaniel should take advantage of first selling a "romance" there for six hundred pounds. If he completed the story of his faun, he could obtain both the money and the English copyright.

The family started on its trip, first to London, but there was too much social life there for Hawthorne to work well. They moved on to Redcar on the coast of Yorkshire.

Redcar was nearly deserted. The brown sands of the beach attracted Hawthorne as he recalled the beaches of his childhood. Each day, he and Julian walked north along the sands; each day Hawthorne heard the throb and beat of the ocean. He was a man of the sea again; he joined his son swimming; he put his own imagination on a sea of adventure. It was at Redcar and at Leamington Spa that he finished *The Marble Faun*, which was called in England *The Transformation*, a title he never liked. After the book received some adverse reviews, he added a chapter to clarify the mystery of the end. He regretted this, as the story was a true romance. He felt his new friend, the historian John Lothrop Motley, understood the book when he wrote:

"Everything you have ever written, I believe, I have read many times, and I am particularly vain of having admired 'Sights from a Steeple,' when I first read it in the Boston 'Token,' several hundred years ago, when we were both younger than we are now; of having detected and cherished, at a later day, 'An Old Apple-Dealer,' whom, I believe, you have unhandsomely thrust out of your presence, now that you are grown so great. But the 'Romance of Monte Beni' has the additional charm for me that it is the first book of yours that I have read since I had the privilege of making your personal acquaintance. My memory goes back at once to those walks (alas, not too frequent) we used to take along the Tiber, or in the Campagna; . . . and it is delightful to get hold of the book now, and know that it is impossible for you any longer, after waving your wand as you occasionally did then, indicating where the treasure was hidden, to sink it again beyond plummet's sound.

"I admire the book exceedingly. . . . It is one which, for the first reading, at least, I didn't like to hear aloud. . . . If I were composing an article for a review, of course, I should feel obliged to show cause for my admiration; but I am only obeying an impulse. Permit me to say, however, that your style seems, if possible, more perfect than ever. Where, O where is the godmother who gave you to talk pearls and diamonds? . . . Believe me, I don't say to you half what I say behind your back; and I have said a dozen times that nobody can write English but you. With regard to the story, which has been somewhat criticised, I can only say that to me it is quite satisfactory. I like those shadowy, weird, fantastic, Hawthornesque shapes flitting through the golden gloom, which is the atmosphere of the book. I like the misty way in which the story is indicated rather than revealed; the outlines are quite definite enough from the beginning to the end to those who have imagination enough to follow you in your airy flights; and to those who complain, I suppose that nothing less than an illustrated edition, with a large gallows on the last page, with Donatello in the most pensile of attitudes—his ears revealed through a white nightcap—would be satisfactory. I beg your pardon for such profanation, but it really moves my spleen that people should wish to bring down the volatile figures of your romance to the level of an every-day romance. . . . The way in which the two victims dance through the Carnival on the last day is very striking. It is like a Greek tragedy in its effect, without being in the least Greek."

Nathaniel answered that the romance had been a success because Motley had been the ideal reader and it did not matter if it ever found another. Incidentally, he wrote, he had booked passage for the United States on June 17. This year of 1860—after seven years in Europe—did not seem promising despite the fact that the United States, rather than Europe, had greeted Hawthorne's *Marble Faun* with real appreciation.

All of the family felt that mixture of excitement and hesitation that travelers who have been long from their country undergo: Would there really be a "welcome home"?

The Marble Faun

 20

"Come in, dear faun," says one of the characters in Hawthorne's extraordinary novel of Italy. The faun, and Italy,
come into the story bringing, as Italy did to Hawthorne,
shadow and sunlight to combine into what we call today a
"Gothic novel." It is curious that *The Marble Faun* is so little
known by young people today. It is a wonderful story, filled
with fantasy, turbulence, an unknown crime, a strange
castle, turrets in the sky, misplaced love, lost love, people in
costume, specters in the night, evil shadows, and through it
all the keen Hawthorne eye observing that country in a fashion so distinct, so clever, and so revealing that Henry James
said, "To know Rome you must go with Hawthorne in your
hands." It is still a remarkable guide.

In England, where he now felt at home, he wrote about the Rome that seemed to compel him to come back, even though he admitted he had no true affection for it. If he did not have affection, he seemed to have an unusual understanding of the city. Rome and the plastic artist went together, Hawthorne felt, and there, for the first time in his life, he had some experience of what it meant to be in an artistic circle. He almost preferred the artists to the writers he knew. The writers, in the end, turned out to be family friends rather than just persons with whom he had intimate intellectual and romantic discussions about the nature of art and artists. Perhaps because he felt he could not and should not deeply examine the motivations of a writer, he had an unusual interest in laying bare some of the heart of the plastic artist in his search for the beautiful. *The Marble Faun*, then, is really about the world of art, the world the artist makes. Hawthorne called it a "romance"—a little shadowy, and then suddenly as bright as the Roman day filled with sunshine.

To show the difference between the Hawthorne of the Notebooks and the Hawthorne of the novel, here is how he describes the Faun of Praxiteles in the novel. Compare its mystery to the casual references in the Notebooks.

"The Faun is the marble image of a young man, leaning his right arm on the trunk or stump of a tree; one hand hangs carelessly by his side; in the other he holds the fragment of a pipe, or some such sylvan instrument of music. His only garment—a lion's skin, with the claws upon his shoulder—falls half-way down his back, leaving the limbs and entire front of his figure nude. The form, thus displayed, is marvellously graceful, but has a fuller and more rounded outline, more flesh, and less of heroic muscle, than the old sculptors were wont to assign to their types of masculine beauty. The character of the face corresponds with the figure; it is most agreeable in outline and feature, but rounded and somewhat voluptuously developed, especially about the throat and chin; the nose is almost straight, but very slightly curves inward, thereby acquiring an indescribable charm of geniality and humor. The mouth, with its full yet delicate lips, seems so nearly to smile outright, that it calls forth a responsive smile. The whole statue—unlike anything else that ever was wrought in that severe material of marble—conveys the idea of an amiable and sensual creature, easy, mirthful, apt for jollity, yet not incapable of being touched by pathos. It is impossible to gaze long at this stone image without conceiving a kindly sentiment towards it, as if its substance were warm to the touch, and imbued with actual life. It comes very close to some of our pleasantest sympathies. . . .

"Only a sculptor of the finest imagination, the most delicate taste, the sweetest feeling, and the rarest artistic skill—in a word, a sculptor and a poet too—could have first dreamed of a Faun in this guise, and then have succeeded in imprisoning the sportive and frisky thing in marble. Neither man nor animal, and yet no monster, but a being in whom both races meet on friendly ground. The idea grows coarse as we handle it, and hardens in our grasp. But, if the spectator broods long over the statue, he will be conscious of its spell; all the pleasantness of sylvan life, all the genial and happy characteristics of creatures that dwell in woods and fields, will seem to be mingled and kneaded into one substance, along with the kindred qualities in the human soul. Trees, grass, flowers, woodland streamlets, cattle, deer, and unsophisticated man. The essence of all these was compressed long ago, and still exists, within that discolored marble surface of the Faun of Praxiteles."

Despite the fact that he did not fully appreciate Rome, there seemed to be something in the city that Hawthorne needed—a new freedom, a new understanding about the past, a new understanding even of his own country. Perhaps it would be too late for Hawthorne to use these elements creatively, but others would come after him, and they would profit from the Americans who had tried to bring the old world and the new world together.

There was a kind of loneliness in Hawthorne's picture of the old world of Italy. He wrote, "In the United States each generation had only its own sins and sorrow to bear," but in the old world it seemed as if "the weary and dreary past were piled upon the back of the present." He was growing homesick, and you find this in the pages of *The Marble Faun*. He would see villagers making wines, for example, and he could not help being reminded of New England and the cider apples: "Our New England vintages where the big piles of golden and rosy apples lie under the orchard trees in the mild autumnal sunshine. . . ." The luscious juice, he said, was finer than wine.

This was the true, the very ancient past that Hawthorne was encountering in Rome. It was this very link to the past and to the sins and sorrows of others that had always interested Hawthorne from the time he was a very young man. His country was beginning now to take on a different aspect from what it once had had in his mind, when all of New England had been painfully tied to the Puritan past, where the sins and crimes that had once reached the ears of Judge Hathorne would ring forever in the memory of Hawthorne's own family.

Despite some somber colors in the pages of *The Marble Faun*, it has in it a glorious light. It is the story of four friends —Donatello, the last surviving member of an ancient Italian family, whose history started with the dawn of civilized time, when a faun had married into it. Through generation after generation, the characteristics of this primitive being would emerge. Donatello, who is gay and frisky and loves to dance, who does not seem to have a sober thought in his head and is unwilling really to think, is the faun of the generation that meets three other friends: Miriam, a strange girl who seems to be without a past; Hilda, a New England girl so pure that she lives with doves in a tower. Hilda herself is not unlike Sophia—she is a copyist and artist, one of the greatest in Rome; she copies the works of great masters. She does not do original work, because there is something in her that allows the great painters to speak through her. There is Kenyon, the American sculptor, often the voice of Hawthorne himself. But all four characters—Donatello, Miriam, Kenyon and Hilda—are the voice of the writer, as characters almost always are in books, giving voice to different facets of an author's personality.

In *The Marble Faun* there are all the ingredients for a good story you want—shadow and sun, love and guilt, hope and despair, the ugly and the beautiful.

It was in September, 1859, that Hawthorne, as was his custom, gave his new book to Sophia for her opinion. He still had not completed the final pages, and it was not until November that she wrote in her diary, "*The Romance of Monte Beni* is completed."

In the story are pictures of many of Hawthorne's friends of the time: faces he had seen, people he had known. Wasn't there a little of Margaret Fuller in Miriam, for example? Margaret Fuller had gone to Rome, married an Italian prince, and died with her husband and young son when they were shipwrecked off the coast of Fire Island as they returned to the United States in 1850. Before she had left America, she had hailed Hawthorne as America's greatest writer, but for Hawthorne she was too aggressive, and when he heard of her death he could only say:

"There never was such a tragedy as her whole story; the sadder and sterner, because so much of the ridiculous was mixed up with it, and because she could bear anything better than to be ridiculous. It was such an awful joke, that she should have resolved—in all sincerity no doubt—to make herself the greatest, wisest, best woman of the age; and, to that end, she set to work on her strange, heavy, unpliable, and, in many respects, defective and evil nature, and adorned it with a mosaic of admirable qualities, such as she chose to possess; putting in here a splendid talent, and there a moral excellence, and polishing each separate piece, and the whole together, till it seemed to shine afar and dazzle all who saw it. She took credit to herself for having been her own Redeemer, if not her own Creator; and, indeed, she was far more a work of art than any of Mr. Mozier's statues. But she was not working on inanimate substance, like marble or clay; there was something within her that she could not possibly come at, to re-create it and refine it; and, by and by, this rude old potency bestirred itself, and undid all her labor in the twinkling of an eye. On the whole, I do not know but I like her the better for it—the better, because she proved herself a very woman, after all, and fell as the weakest of her sisters might."

Hawthorne preferred his women—as did the period—in a role non-competitive with men, and he was always disgruntled with women writers. Frequently his books will divide women into two marked divisions: the good and innocent, and the somewhat wicked and experienced. Only Sophia was the proper woman for him.

Throughout *The Marble Faun* there are glimpses of Hawthorne's life in Italy—the studios and workshops of his artist friends, the landscape of the countryside and of the human heart. Hawthorne called *The Marble Faun* his "moonshiny Romance." It still retains that quality.

Sea Turn

At last they started home. It seemed to all the Hawthornes that they were making a complete circle as they boarded their ship to return to the United States in June, 1860. Wasn't their captain the very captain who had carried them across the sea that hot July morning in 1853, a long seven years ago? It seemed as though everything was the same, yet at the same time as though everything had changed. It was a hot day as they made their way to the ship, and it would be a hot day when they arrived home in Concord.

But things were different. Although their ship was commanded by the good Captain Leitch, who had struck Julian as the greatest of all captains, and was as charming as ever with his bushy black whiskers, the ship was different. The old *Niagara* had long since gone to war. It had been chartered by the British for the war in the Crimea, and once, while Hawthorne was Consul in Liverpool, he and his son had gone down to the wharf to see those red-coated heroes, so many of whom were to die, board on their old paddle-wheel steamer. No, this was a better ship, a fine new ship, and a fine new life seemed on the way.

Harriet Beecher Stowe, the author of that stirring new book, *Uncle Tom's Cabin*, was on board, but Nathaniel found her a little tiresome. She talked entirely too much, and she seemed to want to carry on business when really pleasure was the order of the day on shipboard. James T. Fields and his wife Annie were traveling with the Hawthornes. The greatest of the contemporary publishers, Fields' relationship to the writers of his day was a very intimate one, and Mrs. Harriet Beecher Stowe had decided to give her books to him. Frankly, Mr. Fields, at that point, did not seem to care. He always got hopelessly seasick and resented, but could not help enjoying, the delight that Hawthorne and his family took in the voyage.

Hawthorne's love for the sea amounted to a passionate worship, said Fields, and he himself moaned only that he was the worst sailor on this planet. Yet the voyage was a calm one. Hawthorne said over and over again during those days, quietly, earnestly, as he stood at the railing, "I should like to sail on and on forever, and never touch the shore again."

He particularly liked to stand alone in the ship's bow, and he walked and walked the deck, as some haunted captain of long ago might have. He loved to see the sun go down and the sun come up, and the passengers and his wife Sophia, missing him in the night, could watch him as he walked beneath the stars, almost melancholy, like a lone traveler.

When James Fields was too seasick to come up on deck, Hawthorne tried to amuse him. He explained to Fields that there were all sorts of excellent remedies for seasickness. And, although it didn't help Fields' stomach any, he did amuse the miserable man, and for a while Fields forgot his misery. Hawthorne said to Mr. Fields, for example, that though of course you couldn't eat regular scrambled eggs, you could, while at sea, eat a few roc's eggs beaten up by an appropriate mermaid who would deliver them on a dolphin's back. If you needed strength, then take some of Robin Hood's arrows and make a gruel from them. If you felt really miserable, then perhaps a good stiff cup of hemlock, of the Socrates brand. A dose of salts could be distilled from the tears of Niobe, and potted owl could be made with Minerva sauce. Chicken pies could be made from chickens raised by Mrs. Carey. Nautilus chowder could be made from the sea itself. The main difficulty, said Hawthorne, was that Fields hadn't brought seven-league boots to keep out the damp. "A most satisfactory sea turn," said Fields. The "divine spirit of humor was on Hawthorne those days. . . . I have sailed many a weary, watery mile since then, but Hawthorne was not on board."

This sea voyage took place during a period of transition. Home was still ahead of them, and it was unbearably hot when they stepped out of the train at Concord after arriving in the United States. The entire landscape looked unfamiliar. The fields seemed too brown after the green fields of England. The sun seemed too white and devastating. Concord summers can be oppressive with heat—not even a grasshopper could live, Julian used to say, and he remembered how the water in the river was so warm that when they bathed in it they merely exchanged one form of heat for another.

So this was America's first greeting, this American heat. Hawthorne did not like it, and he did not like what he saw at The Wayside either. They had been living in such large, elaborate homes that The Wayside seemed pathetic. It was painted a dingy buff. A dinginess, too, seemed to them to lay over the land and over the spirit of the people.

Hawthorne and his family, were coming back to a world they had, in a way, left behind, a world that for a while they improperly understood. When Longfellow saw Fields and Hawthorne at the Old Corner Bookshop right after their return, he said they looked like two boys who were going to a "schoolboys' blue Monday." They were suffering not from the transition one makes from one country to another, or from one time to another, or one culture to another, but from their sense that America itself was moving toward disaster.

As Mrs. Harriet Beecher Stowe had said over and over again while crossing the ocean, slavery was shadowing the nation. All Concord had been deeply moved and shocked by the events of October, 1859, when the news came from Harper's Ferry, Virginia, that John Brown had been tried for treason and executed. Brown had been a frequent visitor to Concord and had been looked upon almost as a prophet. Some said he was a fool—he had lived by the sword, and he who lives by it must perish by it. Some said he had thrown his life away. Hawthorne was rather inclined to that opinion. But others spoke of him with the greatest respect: Thoreau, for example, wrote almost secretly in his journal, "I foresee the time when a painter will paint that scene . . . the poet will sing it, the historian record it, and with the landing of the Pilgrims and the Declaration of Independence it will be the ornament of some future national gallery when the present form of slavery shall be no more. We shall then be at liberty to weep for John Brown. Then, and not till then, we will take our revenge. I rejoice that I live in this age, that I was his contemporary."

All that fall, John Brown's death haunted Thoreau. When

he went out to see the sunset, he said, "It was hard for me to see its beauty then when my mind was filled with Captain Brown. So great a wrong as his fate implied overshadowed all beauty in the world."

When John Brown, tried for treason, was finally hanged, the village of Concord held memorial services. Something, thought Henry David Thoreau, had died in his own time. It seemed almost as if John Brown were the only one who had not died.

It was to this world that Hawthorne had returned, a world of grays. There were no sharp delineations between right and wrong. Some thought that Brown had been foolish but, at the same time, that he had also been a patriot. But to Hawthorne, John Brown was simply a fanatic. And, in a way, all Concord was a little confusing to Hawthorne, now temporarily more European than New Englander. The whole world seemed to be in a state of chaos, as was The Wayside, Hawthorne's own home.

The first thing Hawthorne wanted upon his return was a tower study, a tower like those he had known in Rome and in the old palaces of England. He started to build such a tower, a three-story square tower, with windows looking out in all directions, those in front gazing down on Walden Pond.

When the study was completed, Hawthorne tried to put his emotional house in order. First, there was schooling for the children. Julian, for example, now fourteen, must be prepared for Harvard, and he was sent to the school of Mr. Frank Sanborn, who had actually taken a prominent part in the John Brown episode. Hawthorne had been moved by a letter that William Ellery Channing wrote to him describing Sanborn's school. "Our school days are the days of our life," said Channing, perhaps understanding a little of what Hawthorne was feeling. "I'm a little late in welcoming you back to the stern and simple fields of this ancient Puritan land, but a travel is like coffee, it needs to be well settled."

So the settling began. Those who were observant noticed that Hawthorne, who had so dearly loved to walk, was walking much less. Occasionally he went to Walden Pond, a distance of two miles, but mostly he liked to stroll with his family or, more frequently now, with Sophia. They were coming back to an intimacy they had had before the children had consumed so much of their energy. They walked and talked, sharing the beauty of the wood paths.

The first winter after their return imprisoned him, he thought. The drifting snow now seemed strange, the winter unbearably cold. His retreat, his tower with its windows, was almost stifling in the winter because heat from the stove drew the moisture from the air. Each evening, as he had on shipboard, he walked alone, now to the hills, and paced up and down. Once there, he walked back and forth so often that he wore a path, between the huckleberry and sweet fern bushes, beneath the pine. Later he sat in the library reading to his family—from the Bible, and from such contemporary authors as Sir Walter Scott and Tennyson.

Sophia began to be frightened by his lassitude. She could see he was not well. Una had had a recurrence of the Roman fever and now it occurred to her that perhaps Hawthorne, too, had suffered from the same malady while he was in Rome. She tried to be gentle with him, as did his old friends, but time and the coming war proved to be Hawthorne's adversaries.

And soon he lost the companionship of a dear friend, Henry David Thoreau, he who had surveyed the land of The Wayside—"Hawthorne's Estate," he had called it—who had pointed out so many of the beauties of Walden Pond, and who had walked through the Concord woods like a fine, straight Indian. By the time Hawthorne had returned to the United States, Thoreau was ill. Emerson could not imagine a spring without Thoreau going to Saw Mill Brook in search of yellow violets, wading in the water until the plant was discovered. Why, Thoreau could tell what day of the month it was by the very flowers that appeared. Thoreau lingered on for a while, sick and broken, until 1862.

Bronson Alcott was no substitute, in Hawthorne's mind, for Thoreau. Alcott was a good neighbor, perhaps too good, almost over stimulating. The women of the families became extremely intimate: Sophia loved Mrs. Alcott as well as the daughters, Louisa, Elizabeth, and May.

Alcott was now a respected man in Concord, and indeed his interest in schooling had revolutionized the Concord schools. He was now the Superintendent of Schools and received $100 a year. He covered each district, school by school, a journey of some six miles, and he almost overly reported, as they said in those days, to his school committee.

He wanted the best of everything for the children— permanent teachers, teachers' committees, and gatherings of parents. Most important, said Alcott, the child was to have a taste for books, and a town should start building for the future. They must have old books and new books, Hawthorne's *Liberty Tree*, and *Wonder Book* and the *Tanglewood Tales*. The Constitution and the Declaration of Independence should be in every school. And, of course, schools should have newspapers. This idea was totally unheard of in Alcott's day. Schools should teach painting, drawing, gymnastics, dancing, and music—all were necessary for the development of Concord's youth.

But none of his friends supplied the calm or the peace that Hawthorne needed. Indeed, there was no peace now anywhere. The Civil War had broken out. Julian recalled how, in its early days, Hawthorne used to make American history vivid to him by describing all the details of the Revolution. Such history became to Julian "the most vivid and familiar part" of his life.

During that first terrible year, Hawthorne could do no writing. "The present," he said, "the immediate, the actual, has proved too potent for me. It takes away not only my scanty faculty but even my desire for imaginative composition, and leaves me sadly content to scatter a thousand peaceful fantasies upon the hurricane that is sweeping us all along with it."

Sometimes he went into Boston. Perhaps there he would find some peace, particularly at the Old Corner Bookshop, or even at that extraordinary club called The Saturday Club, where Ralph Waldo Emerson, Dr. Oliver Wendell Holmes, James Russell Lowell, and John Greenleaf Whittier met regularly. Hawthorne particularly liked to sit next to Henry Wadsworth Longfellow, a man whom he had grown to admire more and more as time went on.

Longfellow was still suffering from a deep personal loss. He could barely talk about it. In 1861 on a Tuesday afternoon in the hot summer, while his wife was making shields for the children to use in a game, burning wax fell onto her dress; the dress, caught fire. She was cruelly burned and died. Longfellow rarely mentioned his private agony, but once he said, "It was just so with me—I was too happy. I might fancy the gods envied me, if I could fancy heathen gods." His son, Charles Appleton, became a lieutenant in the First Massachusetts Cavalry during the war and was severely wounded in Virginia, as was Holmes's son. Hawthorne found Longfellow a man with a "sense of fitness," and thought there was great charm in his society.

Hawthorne found the same charm in the comfort of his family. He felt then the need for the sea, and he went with Julian to West Beach in Beverly. A letter from Sophia to her husband at this time hints a little of the depression of which Hawthorne had been suffering. "My dearest husband," she writes:

"My babies are a-bed, and I must write down my day to you, or it will not be rounded in. I do not know how to impress you with adequate force concerning the absolutely inspiring effect of thy absence! I have been weighed to the earth by my sense of your depressed energies and spirits, in a way from which I tried in vain to rally. I could not sit down in the house and think about it, and so I kept out as much as possible, at work. For in the house a millstone weighed on my heart and head, and I had to struggle to keep off the bed, where I only fell into a half—a stupid and an unrefreshing—sleep. Of all the trials, this is the heaviest to me—to see you so apathetic, so indifferent, so hopeless, so unstrung. Rome has no sin to answer for so unpardonable as this of wrenching off your wings and hanging lead upon your arrowy feet. Rome—and all Rome caused to you. What a mixed cup is this to drink! My heart's desire has been, ever since the warm days, to get you to the sea under pleasant auspices, in a free and unencumbered way—the sea only, and no people. I saw no way, until this plan of taking Julian occurred to you; and devoutly I blessed God for it, and do now bless Him. I felt so sure that Julian would be only a comfort and a pleasure to you, and am easier to have him with you. It is good for him to be out of the fret of common routine, and it is good for you to have a change from river-damps and sand-heats to ocean fogs and cool sands—and also from the usual days. You especially need *change* of scene and air. I can flourish like purslain anywhere if my heart is at peace. I cannot flourish anywhere if it be not at peace—not in any imaginable Paradise. Well, beloved, you were no sooner fairly gone—it was no sooner half-past eight o'clock—than a great thick cloud rose off my heart and head. I had a thousand things which I meant to do in the house; but Rose wanted me to weed the paths with her while she weeded the beds. So I took advantage of the shaded sun and went out. First she took a small basket and I took a big one, and we went down into the garden to get potatoes and squashes. I gathered four squashes, and she got a basket nearly full of potatoes. Then we weeded."

Julian remembered those days happily in *Pride's Crossing* the fresh sea perch or bass that father and son had so often for dinner; the superb swimming. One could afford to neglect the news. Hawthorne knew this neighborhood from his childhood, and he told Julian many stories of local traditions.

Hawthorne still kept in touch by mail with many old friends who had been associated with his life on the docks, and he, in turn, received touching letters from old workers. One, James Oakes, for example, wrote from the Long Wharf, Boston, on October 8, 1861:

"My Dear Sir,—I took the liberty of sending you this morning a paper containing a view of the exterior of my old store, but forgot to tell you that I have been on Long Wharf forty years!—thirty-one of which I have been an occupant of the old store. There are old gray-head spiders still here with whom I have been acquainted for nearly twenty years, and *you* can well understand that we have become well acquainted with each other. Pray drop in and see the old fellows. I doubt not they will recognize you as an old friend.— Always sincerely yours, James Oakes."

But Hawthorne did not drop in to see his old friends on the wharves. He was too tired and too listless, and the war was too pervasive.

The Mouth of the War

❧ 22 ❧

"Louisa goes into the very mouth of the war." So said Sophia
on a cold December day in 1862. Louisa was determined to
become a nurse. It seemed to Sophia that the events of the
war had drawn her into more and more activity. She would
go over later to the Alcotts' and help Mrs. Alcott mark
Louisa's clothes with indelible ink. Louisa was upstairs pack-
ing all her Dickens, together with as many games as she could
find in what had once been the household of *Little Women*.

One suppertime, Julian Hawthorne came home and told
his mother that the big battle had at last begun: Fredericks-
burg was on fire. During the days, Nathaniel Hawthorne
had secreted himself in his tower. He had tried to write and
had pulled down all the blinds to achieve a darkness to match

the darkness of his spirit. Later he had run into Dr. Oliver Wendell Holmes, "the autocrat of the breakfast table," and Holmes, as usual, had a great deal to say.

That day he talked about war and newspapers. The newspaper, said Holmes, had become as important as bread to the country. Everyone was sick, he said; "we live on our emotions, and in a time of war those emotions go haywire. For example," Holmes also wrote on the subject, "there is a natural war fever. Oh, surely there is patriotism, but, in addition to that, feelings during wartime were kindled with fuel of all sorts, the love of adventure, the contagion of example, the fear of losing the chance of participating in the great adventure of the time, the desire of personal distinction." It was a time of restlessness.

"Men could not write today," said Holmes, "or think, or even attend to their ordinary business. Do you notice how they go up and down the streets and saunter out upon the public places?" Holmes, who knew Hawthorne had put down some of his work when the war broke out and was having difficulty returning to it, tried to reassure him. He knew a scholar, for example, who had fallen into such a state that he would read the same newspaper telegram dispatches over and over again until he felt as if he were an idiot.

War was an old story, but to the generation of Hawthorne and Holmes, civil war was a new one. Surely they all remembered tales of the Revolution. Holmes, for example, remembered that his mother had lost her doll and had never forgotten that important event in relation to the Revolution. Hawthorne, when he had lived in the Old Manse, had often walked beside the burial ground of the British soldiers by the North Bridge.

Those walks stirred something in his mind. The Revolution and his feelings about the Civil War began to merge in a book, *Septimius Felton,* in which a young man kills another at the beginning of the Revolution and thereby discovers a paper that explains some of the secrets of eternal life, how to make an elixir of immortality.

Hawthorne used to watch Julian pretending to be a soldier. He was too young for this war, and Hawthorne thanked God it would be over before he would be old enough to serve. Sophia didn't seem to be as disturbed as he by the turn of events. Quite the contrary, she seemed to be delighted now to be with her sisters once again, doing, as did all the Peabody girls, so much good.

When Sophia and Nathaniel returned from England after their long European stay, Sophia discovered that she was quite out of touch with her sisters. For their part, Mary and Elizabeth felt almost alienated from Sophia. Mary had lost her husband, Horace Mann, and had come to Concord, where, for a few months, she stayed at The Wayside, awaiting her sister's return. She felt miserable there, however; the only time she felt at all comfortable was when she was walking up and down compulsively along the path Hawthorne had made behind the house.

Her brother, Nathaniel Peabody, now known as Dr. Peabody in Concord, was also in the village. Perhaps she should stay on in Concord, thought Mary, and she found a house that she liked immediately, one that she and Elizabeth could certainly live in. Libby, of course, was still trying to change the world. "I may do something satisfactory to myself and friends which I have not done before," she said, and when Mary started her school in Concord, Elizabeth did much to help.

Both of the Peabody sisters had felt the execution of John Brown keenly. Elizabeth had collected money for Brown when he had come to visit Alcott. Later, she had gone to Richmond, Virginia, to try to obtain a reprieve for one of the men who had accompanied Brown at Harper's Ferry. So much had happened in the United States that Libby tried to keep Sophia informed while she was in Europe. And not only Sophia; she wanted Una, her niece, who was nearly sixteen by that time, to know about justice and injustice, to know about slavery and what should truly be freedom. She tried to explain all this in letters that Una could understand. She asked if Una were reading the newspapers, but Sophia, strangely enough, was keeping Una not only from the newspapers but from a good part of the world itself.

"Your whole story is very interesting," Sophia used to write back to Elizabeth, "though I do not agree to some of your doctrines." As time went on, it appeared that Sophia did not believe in many of the doctrines in which Elizabeth and Mary believed.

People turned against Hawthorne because Franklin Pierce, the former President, had been a Copperhead, not supporting Northern attitudes in the Civil War. Hawthorne, of course, was against slavery, but he had become so much of a recluse that few people really knew his position about the war.

As the war went on, Sophia did her share. Not only did she mark Louisa May Alcott's clothes, but she tried to give comfort and affection to those in Concord whose sons had gone to war. There were bandages to be made for the wounded, and Sophia did more than her part. She painted pictures to be given away at the Fair at which money was raised for the Union troops. She comforted her husband, understood her children, and tried to keep from dejection herself.

And she once again became friends with her sisters. They would never thoroughly understand one another, but at least now they were all working for the common good.

It even looked as if Hawthorne himself were working well again. He had taken all the diaries of his English journey and had written a series of brilliant essays called "Our Old

Home." They are still some of the best examples of the essay form in American literature. His disparaged them, though, because the material he chose to work from was not fresh and new. He started books and laid them down, thought of ideas, would play with them a little, and then abandon them. He grew more and more worried that he would never write satisfactorily again, that his health would never be truly up to the long battle a sustained work of literature must be. The war had taken away that inner security he needed, the security he always said was so important to him to be able to work carefully and at length.

The entire war seemed telescoped. Was it just a year ago that Louisa had gone away to be a nurse at the battlefront? Now she was back. Her father had to fetch her after she had contracted a terrible fever. The two ran into Una Hawthorne as they boarded the train for Concord. During the entire trip, Louisa rested her head on Una's shoulder. She looked ghastly and rolled her eyes. She seemed, thought Una, an absolute sheet of flame, and Una, remembering her own Roman fever, tried to comfort her in every way she could, but she was a little frightened, too; this fever seemed so powerful. It was probably diphtheria, and we know now that it was possible that Una and other members of her family had had diphtheria in years gone by. At any rate Una though exposed to Louisa, did not contract the fever.

It was a long, painful time before Louisa recovered. When the Hawthorne women and Julian, too, went over to see her, she had no gay stories to regale them with. But, bit by bit, Louisa began to relate the true story of the war, the story of death and suffering and of the soldiers she had known.

"They were all so young," she said, "so young and so sorely wounded." They used to follow her with their pale faces and watchful eyes full of awe. The nights were the worst. Then she would watch the soldiers trying so painfully to breathe, those terrible breaths, because the musket balls had so pierced lung and rib, so broken and wounded the soldiers, that there was no chance they might live. She used to hover over them, doing what she could, bathing their faces, brushing their hair, smoothing their pillows.

Occasionally she would put heliotropes on their fresh bed linen. They would watch her making little nosegays that she would hand out with sheer delight. She would write their letters. "Shall it be addressed to wife or mother, John?" "Neither, Ma'am," they replied, "I've got no wife and will write to mother myself when I get better." But they never got better. She watched them as they grew more and more dumb, their lips paler and paler, and many, too many, held her hand as they died. She would stop talking then, her eyes staring off in space.

For nearly a year Louisa was in an acute depression. She no longer read Dickens to the village children or played games with them.

Somewhere she was going over in her mind all the activities of the war, and finally they came tumbling out in a book called *Hospital Sketches*. It was one of the most successful books of the war. Louisa caught the spirit of loneliness, alienation, pain, homesickness, and misery of that terrible conflict, and the book started her on a literary career that was to culminate in a few years in a book that went around the world and through history, *Little Women*.

The Hawthorne children saw the Emerson children as well as the Alcotts, and there were a few simple parties where word games abounded. Nonsense verses were growing popular in those days, and Julian particularly delighted in one that applied to him. He had made a journey with his father, and it was his father who insisted they return home because "it would be impossible for us to stay longer than 'til a week from tomorrow because Julian's breeches are in such terrible disrepair, what with bushes, briars, swamps, rocks, beach, mud, seawater, and vicious hard usage and mischances. I struggled hard to prevent him from spoiling his light trousers because if he spoils them he will be inevitably compelled to stay in bed all summer." From that incident his father wrote:

> "There was an old Boy, with a new coat and breeches,
> Who jumped over fences, and tumbled in ditches,
> While the mud and the mire,
> Spattered higher and higher,
> Till he went to the fire,
> And, as he grew drier,
> Burnt great holes in his new coat and breeches."

Occasionally, such nonsense verses would apply to life in Concord—specifically, to neighbors. One applied to Mr. Alcott, whose daughters regularly came over to play cards, but whom Hawthorne himself rarely saw.

> "There dwelt a Sage at Apple-Slump,
> Whose dinner never made him plump;
> Give him carrots, potatoes, squash, parsnips, and peas,
> And some boiled macaroni, without any cheese,
> And a plate of raw apples to hold on his knees,
> And a glass of sweet cider to wash down all these—
> And he'd prate of the Spirit as long as you'd please,—
> This airy Sage of Apple Slump!"

Alcott was still talking about the Spirit, discussing it, lecturing about it, wanting to expand it in all directions. The Spirit of New England, the Spirit of Time, the Spirit of New Civilization, the Spirit of Education. But Hawthorne's enthusiasm for this kind of talk seemed to be disappearing. It was winter and he knew it was his best time for work; he had just finished the *English Sketches.* "But somehow," he said "there is something preternatural in my reluctance to begin. I linger at the threshold." "You ought to be thankful," he wrote to his publisher, "that, like most other broken down authors, I do not pester you with decrepit pages. Seriously, my mind has, for the present, lost its temper and its fine edge, and I have an instinct that I had better keep quiet."

Hawthorne tried to write during these last years, but nothing came to fruition. *Septimius Felton* existed in two different versions; then there was *Dr. Grimshawe's Secret* and another unfinished manuscript called *The Ancestral Footsteps,* which he had started in Italy. Both had as their theme the Americans' refusal to accept an English cultural inheritance.

Hawthorne tried to understand the American writer's feeling toward his origin in English literature. He had, as did his friend Herman Melville, a great sympathy for the man who had lost his roots. He remembered two things that had happened when he was in the Consulate. Many had come to ask his help with their claims to some English estate that might or might not be imaginary. And others came simply because they wanted to get home. One old man, rather like Melville's character, Israel Potter, was particularly fascinating to Hawthorne. "His manner and accent," he said, "did not quite convince me that he was an American, and I told him so; but he steadfastly affirmed—'Sir, I was born and lived in 92nd Street, Philadelphia,' and then went on to describe some public edifices and other local objects with which he used to be familiar, adding with the simplicity that touched me very closely, 'Sir, I had rather be there than here! . . .'"

Hawthorne himself was back on his own soil, but the soil in some parts of the eastern seaboard was literally stained with blood, the blood of civil war. Hawthorne worked too, at this point, on *Septimius Felton,* the story of an elixir of life, a liquid that would give one immortality. He based such

a scene on the story that Thoreau had told them about The
Wayside and the man who lived there and thought he would
never die.

Despite the fact that he could not write easily, he was still
happy visiting the people who understood him best, he
thought: his publishers. W. D. Ticknor, Fields's partner,
was a particularly fine friend. He had sent Hawthorne the
special cider he had so longed for when he was in Italy.
Franklin Pierce came frequently, as did many contributors
to the *Atlantic*—young William Dean Howells, for example,
who wanted to go west. Such an idea momentarily aroused
Hawthorne's enthusiasm. What would it be like, he thought,
to go to some section of the country that did not have the
burden of the past or of Europe resting upon it?

He met, and very much enjoyed, Miss Gail Hamilton,
who stayed at the Hawthornes' and wrote afterwards, "He is
a glorious man, a very ideal man in his personal appearance
with an infinite forehead, his gray, dry, long hair thrown
back from it in all directions, deep lamps of eyes growing out
from under their heavy arches, black eyebrows and mus-
tache. . . . He talks little, but he talks extremely well."

Ticknor and Fields, who were the publishers of Hawthorne's work, delighted him by bringing out a new edition
of Sir Walter Scott and also a new edition of Lockhart's *Life
of Scott*, which they dedicated to Hawthorne. Books now
were a great comfort to him. Julian remembered how pleasant it was to see him sitting with a book. "He would settle
himself comfortably in his chair and hold the book open in
his left hand, his fingers clasping it over the top, and as he
read there was a constant recurring forward movement of his
head which would seem somehow to give distinctness and
significance to the sentences and paragraphs, and indicated a
constant, living rapport between him and the author."

James Fields and his wife were especially warm to him.

He enjoyed visiting them at their fashionable literary gatherings on Charles Street in Boston. But, even more, he enjoyed visiting them in Beverly, where they might have a gigantic clam bake that brought him back to the days of his boyhood.

During one of his periods of despair, Fields had arranged for Hawthorne to go to Washington and write about President Lincoln and some of the affairs of state. The result was an article, "Chiefly About War Matters," which was later published in the *Atlantic Monthly*. That year he sat for a portrait and many photographs. He wrote home, "My hair is not really so white. The sun seems to take an infernal pleasure in making me venerable as if I were as old as himself." In another letter home, he wrote:

"I have never a moment's time to write, for I move about all day, and am engaged all the evening; and if ever there is a vacant space, I want to employ it in writing my journal, which keeps terribly behindhand. But I suppose mamma and the rest of you sometimes remember there is such a person, and wish to know what I am about. I went up yesterday to Harper's Ferry (a distance of eighty miles from Washington) by invitation of the directors of a railroad; so that I made the whole journey without expense, and partook of two cold collations besides. To be sure, I paid my expenses with a speech; but it was a very short one. I shall not describe what I saw, because very likely I shall print it in the 'Atlantic Monthly;' but I made acquaintance with some rebel prisoners, and liked them very much. It rained horribly all day, and the mud was such as nobody in New England can conceive of. I have shaken hands with Uncle Abe, and have seen various notabilities, and am infested by people who want to exhibit me as a lion. . . ."

Even his publisher thought that Hawthorne had not given the proper respect to Abraham Lincoln. Some of the paragraphs were omitted, much to Hawthorne's embarrassment and annoyance, because the publisher said they were of no historical interest. But they were published after Hawthorne's and Lincoln's deaths and were, just as Hawthorne had maintained, of great historical interest.

Hawthorne received some unfavorable letters because of his less than worshipful attitude toward Lincoln. He received even more when he dedicated his book *Our Old Home* to Franklin Pierce. He had dedicated it to him out of friendship —if it hadn't been for Pierce, he would never have gone to England and would never have written the book. But many people turned on him cruelly. Harriet Beecher Stowe was shocked that the book had been published at all. Unfavorable opinions were expressed behind his back. He grew more isolated and alone.

Hawthorne needed money, and yet he could not write. But Ticknor and Fields made every effort to pay him for anything he did. When the Hawthornes had left Liverpool, they had saved a large amount of money, but now there was inflation and money did not go very far. The book business, too, looked as if it were going to be in sorry shape.

Hawthorne longed for a change. He was always longing for a change, as though changing his environment would somehow change or relieve some of the pain and anguish inside himself. If he could only go to the sea, he would be happy. Why hadn't he built his tower by the sea, instead of in Concord? Now Concord began to seem a little alien to him, except for his walks behind the house or on the hills.

His friends, particularly Longfellow, tried to cheer him up. Longfellow proposed a dinner for Hawthorne, a small one, just "two sad authors and two jolly publishers—nobody else." Hawthorne had a kind of majesty about him in those days; his long cap, his white hair, his dark eyes made him look almost like some defeated general of literature, some captain of the imagination whose ship was slowly sinking beneath him.

When Franklin Pierce's wife died in December of 1863, Hawthorne went with Pierce to New Hampshire. He was always comfortable with Pierce—their boyhood at school had established a bond that lasted their entire lives. When he returned, he stopped in at Charles Street, in the Fields's drawing room; and once again his memory seemed to revolve more around his boyhood and his college years than around the present. Books were important again. He was rereading Boswell, delighting in him all over again—surely he was one of the most remarkable men of all times. He talked about neighbors; the Sage of Apple Slump was not exactly easy to live with, and Mrs. Alcott herself was a woman always eager to tell stories of doom and disaster about the war. He was intensely witty, said Annie Fields, but his wit was of an ethereal texture. "He would sit," she said, "in the ample chimney and look at the stars through the great aperture. 'Ah,' he said, 'how well I recall the summer days also, when with my gun, I roamed at will through the woods of Maine. How sad middle life looks to people of erratic temperaments. Everything is beautiful in youth, for all things are allowed to it then.' "

A Cruel Journey

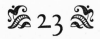 23

"Why does nature treat us like little children?" There was a querulous note in Hawthorne's voice as he sat again in the living room of James and Annie Fields, his beloved publishers. They were startled to hear the hint of desperation. The light in Hawthorne's eyes was as beautiful as ever, but his legs seemed to have shrunk. He was no longer the giant in literature but almost a little child. The vigor was completely gone, and he did not seem to hear what others were saying. "I think we could bear it all," Hawthorne continued, "if we knew our fate." He hesitated and then said, "At least it would not make much difference to me now what became of me."

The Fieldses tried to cheer him, and they succeeded to a

degree. By evening he had brightened up a little as they talked of the touch of spring that was delicately influencing the end of March. The literary people of Boston were well aware of the spring, and the pages of the *Atlantic Magazine,* which was now owned by Fields and Ticknor, rejoiced in each new season. They spoke of squirrels peeking out of their holes, of sudden bluebirds. Robins had made their first appearance. Sparrows, blackbirds, and wild pigeons were beginning to appear. You might run across a fly, perhaps, a grasshopper, a butterfly, a snake, or a turtle. Wild geese had started to go northward. Soon the frogs would begin croaking.

The Fieldses thought it was good that Hawthorne had gotten through the winter. Nature may treat us like little children, he said, but it also gave us the spring to try to recover.

Annie Fields always seemed to bring out Hawthorne's wit, and he began a few of his delightful anecdotes about other days. But suddenly he would stop himself, look out over the water, seeing how it sparkled in the moonlight. So had the moonlight sparkled as he had viewed it from so many homes he had known; over the harbor in Salem, over Walden Pond as he saw it from his tower in Concord, over the rivers in Maine, over all the coast of New England, it seemed. He said suddenly that the moon, as one got older, lost its charm.

The Fieldses looked at each other; they began to wonder about Hawthorne. They had heard, for example, that he had stopped by the Emerson home one night, and that the Emerson teenagers had shown him pictures, some lantern slides of Concord scenes very familiar to Hawthorne, but that he had not seemed to recognize them at all.

As the Fieldses and Hawthorne sat there in the living room, England seemed closer to him than the United States, and yet he was not content with England. The British had not liked the portrait he had painted in *Our Old Home.* "The extent over which her dominions have spread," he complained, "leads her to fancy herself stronger than she really is, but she is not today a powerful empire, she is much like a squash vine which runs over a whole garden, but if you cut it at the root it is at once destroyed."

Those words certainly were more than a little prophetic in terms of what was to happen to the British Empire in the years to come. But that evening with the Fieldses Hawthorne did not dwell on any one subject; his mind seemed torn and chaotic, just as his legs seemed weak and unable to support the little strength his body contained.

Hawthorne seemed more cheerful at breakfast with the Fieldses. All of his Concord neighbors were kind, he said, and Alcott was really one of the most excellent men he had ever known. He could well see why Emerson had been so delighted with him over the years and at the same time so irritated with him. It was impossible to quarrel with Alcott, for he would take all your harsh words like a saint.

Sophia knew that Hawthorne enjoyed traveling and urged him to go on a trip with Ticknor. In a way it was similar to the journeys he had taken as a boy, when he got on a stagecoach and did not know whom he would see, where he would go, but just went on and on collecting new experiences and new stories. Now his mind did not seem alert enough for any story, his body too weak to savor any sensation. He was curiously self-centered. "If I could but get to England now I think that the sea voyage might set me aright." So he started off on what Ticknor hoped would be a sea voyage to Cuba.

Their first stop was the Astor House in New York. In the old days, Hawthorne would have loved the Astor, associated as it was with so many noted men and so near the homes of people he admired as writers. Washington Irving, for example, had just moved into a house down the street. The

Astor House was known for its oysters, and Hawthorne, when he could eat nothing else in those final years, longed for oysters. His good friend was careful about writing home to Mrs. Hawthorne. She pleaded for good news.

A northeaster had driven down on New York. In the old days Hawthorne would have been out walking and dreaming in such weather. But today he said he just needed rest. The next day Ticknor wrote again to Sophia, "Mr. Hawthorne is improving, I trust. I hope the sun will appear tomorrow that we may see something of New York." Hawthorne was sleeping well, and the following day he was even better. He received a letter from Mrs. Hawthorne. "I handed it to our King," said Ticknor, "and he read it with interest and delight." He took a long walk and everything seemed fine. The friends rode around in a hansom cab. They saw Central Park, and Hawthorne spent an enjoyable evening.

They made their way to Philadelphia, Hawthorne not going out because the weather continued poor, but at least he took an interest in the papers, and they had some pleasant drives. "I tell him we will float along and see 'what turns up,'" wrote Ticknor, but a trip by sea was out of the question because of the storm, which had persisted.

That was the last letter Ticknor wrote. With everyone solicitous and watchful of Hawthorne, so careful of everything from his diet to his state of mind, no one had recognized, least of all Nathaniel Hawthorne, that Ticknor himself was suffering from a dangerous cold. The cold evidently had become much more serious than anyone realized, and there, in Philadelphia, away from the Boston he loved and the friends he knew, with only a sick man as a companion, W. D. Ticknor died.

The effect on Hawthorne was catastrophic. He knew no one. There was no one to whom he could turn. He was able to telegraph home the news, and Mr. Ticknor's son came down to handle further arrangements.

When Sophia saw Nathaniel next, she was shocked and frightened. He was so haggard, so white, so deeply scored with pain and fatigue, she said, that his face was more ill than she had ever seen it. In his confusion, misery, and despair, Hawthorne had walked from the Concord station, and the effort in the April warmth had been almost too much for him. He had not allowed himself to feel anything, said Sophia, and now he must give way if he needed to. He could barely sit up, and he lay on the couch. He did not wish to be read to, and he did not seem to be able to fix his thoughts at all.

After a day or two, he was asked if he could come in to his Saturday Club, the great literary club of Boston where they were celebrating the bicentennial of Shakespeare. Sophia said gently, "He could as easily build London as go to the Shakespeare dinner." But all this time Hawthorne maintained that when the wind was warm he would feel well again. It was the cold wind that was ruining him.

Sophia longed for him to go to Cuba or some island in the Gulf Stream. "He is my world and all the business of it," she said. She made him laugh finally by reading Thackeray to him, but it was a smile that looked strange on a face that once shone like "a thousand suns with smiles." The only thing that would make him happy would be another trip, she thought. General Pierce would take him.

They would wait until May and then start out.

The Unfinished Window

❧ 24 ❧

Sophia had kept closely in touch with Julian, now at Harvard, but Julian was not fully aware of how his father's health had deteriorated until one day when he came to Concord from Cambridge to see him. Nathaniel was sitting in the upstairs bedroom with his wife and children. It was a pleasant May day. Julian wanted to go on a class trip, and his father said he might. He had to take an afternoon train back. It was the only one that could return him to college in time, but he lingered, looking at his father.

"I said good-bye," he wrote, "and went to the door where I stood a moment looking back into the room. He was standing at the foot of the bed, leaning against it and looking at me with a smile. He had on his old dark coat, his hair was almost wholly white, he was very pale. But the expression on his face was full of beautiful kindness, the kindness of having given his son a pleasure, and perhaps something more that I did not then know of. His aspect at that moment, and the sunshine on the little room, are vivid in my memory. I never saw my father again."

By the middle of May, Hawthorne seemed well enough to start his trip to Plymouth, New Hampshire. As always, he took a notebook with him, but the handwriting had almost become illegible by this time, and, where once there had been long pages of detailed description, rapid characterizations of the people he saw, myriads of ideas for books, there were now only a few words entered at the end of each day. Hawthorne was tired and went to bed early. Pierce took a room next to him and left the door open. Hawthorne was sleeping soundly.

At midnight, Pierce heard a howling dog in the courtyard of the hotel and went to check his friend. He found that his heart had stopped beating.

It was the twenty-third of May in the year 1864 when Hawthorne, just short of being sixty years old, was buried in the Sleepy Hollow Cemetery of Concord. First they carried him through the blossoming orchards and then put him down gently under a group of pines overlooking, as Fields said, "this historic field of Concord."

The next day Emerson wrote in his journal: "May 24: Yesterday, May 23, we buried Hawthorne in Sleepy Hollow, in a pomp of sunshine and verdure, and gentle winds. James Freeman Clarke read the service in the church and at the grave. Longfellow, Lowell, Holmes, Agassiz, Hoar, Dwight, Whipple, Norton, Alcott, Hillard, Fields, Judge Thomas, and I attended the hearse as pallbearers. Franklin

Pierce was with the family. . . . All was so bright and quiet that pain or mourning was hardly suggested, and Holmes said to me that it looked like a happy meeting.

"Clarke in the church said that Hawthorne had done more justice than any other to the shades of life, shown a sympathy with the crime in our nature, and, like Jesus, was the friend of sinners.

"I thought there was a tragic element in the event, that might be more fully rendered—in the painful solitude of the man, which, I suppose, could not longer be endured, and he died of it.

"I have found in his death a surprise and disappointment. I thought him a greater man than any of his works betray, that there was still a great deal of work in him, and that he might one day show a purer power. Moreover, I have felt sure of him in his neighborhood, and in his necessities of sympathy and intelligence—that I could well wait his time—his unwillingness and caprice—and might one day conquer a friendship. It would have been a happiness, doubtless to both of us, to have come into habits of unreserved intercourse. It was easy to talk with him—there were no barriers—only, he said so little, that I talked too much, and stopped only because, as he gave no indications, I feared to exceed. He showed no egotism or self-assertion, rather a humility, and, at one time, a fear that he had written himself out. One day, when I found him on the top of his hill, in the woods, he paced back the path to his house, and said, 'This path is the only remembrance of me that will remain.' Now it appears that I waited too long."

The path, of course, was not the only remembrance of Hawthorne that remained. His wife and children were inspired by him throughout their lives. Sophia wrote later:

". . . Everything noble, beautiful, and generous in his action Mr. Hawthorne hid from himself, even more cunningly than he hid himself from others. He positively never contemplated the best thing he could do as in the slightest degree a personal matter; but somehow as a small concordance with God's order—a matter of course. It was almost impossible to utter to him a word of commendation. He made praise show absurd and out of place, and the praiser a mean blunderer; so perfectly did everything take its true place before him. The flame of his eyes consumed compliment, cant, sham, and falsehood, while the most wretched sinners—so many of whom came to confess to him—met in his glance a pity and sympathy so infinite, that they ceased to be afraid of God, and began to return to Him. In his eyes, as Tennyson sings, 'God and Nature met in Light.' So that he could hardly be quarrelled with for veiling himself from others, since he veiled himself from himself. His own soul was behind the wings of the cherubim,—sacred, like all souls which have not been desecrated by the world. I never dared to gaze at him, even I, unless his lids were down. It seemed an invasion into a holy place. To the last, he was in a measure to me a divine mystery; for he was so to himself. I have an eternity, thank God, in which to know him more and more, or I should die in despair. Even now I progress in knowledge of him, for he informs me constantly."

Hawthorne's works, said Oliver Wendell Holmes, would keep his name "in remembrance as long as the language in which he shaped his deep imaginations is spoken by human life." James Russell Lowell proclaimed that Hawthorne had the rarest creative imagination of the century, probably the rarest since Shakespeare.

Hawthorne has grown increasingly important since the year of his death. He is remembered not only by that path behind his home but by all paths, because indeed his very steps in his novels and essays were paths in the beautiful country of what was called the American Renaissance in literature.

It is true that Hawthorne's life, as most lives are, was a little unfinished, his perhaps more than many writers because his writing power in his last years had been struck down as cruelly as his strength. The unfinished *Dolliver Romance*, on which he was working when he died, was laid, together with a little nosegay of snowflowers, on his coffin. Longfellow, his boyhood friend, wrote a poem about Hawthorne's death that was soon known throughout New England.

> How beautiful it was, that one bright day
>   In the long week of rain!
> Though all its splendor could not chase away
>   The omnipresent pain.
>
> The lovely town was white with apple-blooms,
>   And the great elms o'erhead
> Dark shadows wove on their aerial looms,
>   Shot through with golden thread.
>
> Across the meadows, by the gray old manse,
>   The historic river flowed:—
> I was as one who wanders in a trance,
>   Unconscious of his road.
>
> The faces of familiar friends seemed strange;
>   Their voices I could hear,
> And yet the words they uttered seemed to change
>   Their meaning to the ear.
>
> For the one face I looked for was not there,
>   The one low voice was mute;
> Only an unseen presence filled the air,
>   And baffled my pursuit.

Now I look back, and meadow, manse, and stream
　　Dimly my thought defines;
I only see—a dream within a dream—
　　The hill-top hearsed with pines.

I only hear above his place of rest
　　Their tender undertone,
The infinite longings of a troubled breast,
　　The voice so like his own.

There in seclusion and remote from men
　　The wizard hand lies cold,
Which at its topmost speed let fall the pen,
　　And left the tale half told.

Ah, who shall lift that wand of magic power,
　　And the lost clue regain?
The unfinished window in Aladdin's tower
　　Unfinished must remain!

The *Dolliver Romance* did remain unfinished, but in its pages the old Hawthorne, the powerful captain of the imagination, was once more in control after he had seemed to have lost his way in a fog of illness and depression. Hawthorne was truly a window, now an unfinished window but a window on the American present, and as such, as one of the great spirits of the American Renaissance, his truth, as they said of John Brown, goes marching on.

Hawthorne's truth was, of course, as he described it, "the truth of the human heart." In these words he showed that he understood some of the idosyncrasies of the human heart, and we can be justified in calling him the first American psychological novelist. It wasn't until the twentieth century, when Freud and other great minds began to understand the strange, uncharted seas of the unconscious, that writers such as Hawthorne were appreciated with a new vigor.

Hawthorne had charted many of the coasts and streams and deep waters that writers who were to come after him would try to explore. Many of them would do it more pompously and pretentiously; few had the sympathy, tolerance, or genius to make of their stories both great reading and great essays in understanding as well.

Today, Hawthorne is read as much as he was read in that first period of success he enjoyed after the years of neglect. There are more books about Hawthorne being published than almost any other American writer. He is appreciated and enjoyed in England and on the Continent because his eagerness to explore the human soul is a universal eagerness, just as the human soul itself is a universal quality in all of us.

He was, then, our first psychological novelist. He was, too, our greatest Gothic novelist—a novel form that today becomes of greater and greater interest to young people. Also, as the science-fiction novel begins to explore other worlds, we must realize that Hawthorne was one of the first writers to explore that field. He was always interested in the Gothic, always fascinated by the supernatural, always attracted to the effect of science upon character. *Rappacini's Daughter*, until its last fragment, was concerned with the wonder of the day in which man might increase his time on earth, or, at least, his understanding.

Hawthorne consistently showed an understanding heart, and that is the real key to the richness of life. Today, when the novel has taken all sorts of strange and ambiguous paths, the writer who dares to say that his territory and the chart he follows is the path of the human heart is as brave as a man about to explore the moon.

We must remember, too, that, in the nineteenth century,

emotions were as little explored as are the contours of the moon today. Hawthorne could see that good and bad existed in the same person, that, try as one might, he would occasionally take the wrong path leading to, his own and to others' destruction.

Hawthorne was born at a time when the novel was in the process of change. He had to create and shape his own image, and, in so doing, he carved and sharpened many of the facets of American literature. Just as he molded the story *Drowne's Wooden Image* so that a woodcarver's masterpiece appears to be a robot, so he opened the way to the paths of science fiction, the Gothic, the psychological novel, and, greater than all of these, perhaps, the romance. He combined, said Henry James, "spontaneity of the imagination with a haunting care for moral problems. Man's conscience was his theme, but he saw it in the light of the creative fancy."

In his own time, writers such as Henry James realized Hawthorne was original and important. We read him today; he is still original, still important; he guides us in the byways of the human heart, in some of the fascinating history of early New England, in the mystery and suspense of our own past, and in the pleasures of our immediate present. He is still great reading, and he is still a great part of our American heritage.

Emerson had said that Concord in his time was at a period in which "high tides are caused in the human spirit." Hawthorne knew both the high tide and the ebb tide of the human spirit. He was the first great captain of the American imagination.

Appendix

Important Dates in the Life
of Nathaniel Hawthorne

1804: Nathaniel Hawthorne was born on July 4th in Salem, Massachusetts. He was the son of a sea captain, Nathaniel, and of Elizabeth Clark Manning Hathorne. The couple had two other children, one an older girl and the other a younger girl. Both his mother's family, the Mannings, and his father's, the Hathornes, were descended from early and important New England settlers.

1808: Captain Nathaniel Hathorne died in Surinam, Dutch Guiana, on the coast of South America. He left his family in poor straits, and they became at least partially dependent on the Mannings, the family of Mrs. Hathorne.

1809: Nathaniel, his mother, and two sisters moved to the Manning house on Herbert Street in Salem.

1813–
1815:
Nathaniel Hawthorne injured his foot, probably twice, according to the most recent scholarship. In any case, his reading was greatly encouraged and his physical activity greatly reduced. Nathaniel Hawthorne, his sisters, and his mother went to live on the land inherited from the Mannings at Raymond, Maine.

1819:
Nathaniel Hawthorne returned in the summer to Salem to study in Samuel Archer's school.

1820:
Nathaniel Hawthorne studied under the brilliant teacher, Benjamin L. Oliver, in Salem. In the late summer and fall of that year, he began to publish *The Spectator,* a paper written, printed, and distributed by him. His mother and his sisters returned to Salem at this time.

1821–
1825:
Nathaniel Hawthorne attended Bowdoin College in Brunswick, Maine. Among his famous classmates were Henry Wadsworth Longfellow and Franklin Pierce.

1825:
In the year 1825 Nathaniel Hawthorne began his long stay in the "chamber under the eaves" in Salem. For nearly a dozen years he lived a life of solitude, developing his skill as a writer.

1825:
Nathaniel Hawthorne brought out his first published novel at his own expense. It was published anonymously. He was dissatisfied with the book, however, and destroyed all copies he could acquire throughout his lifetime.

1828:
In the fall of 1828 he traveled to New Haven, Connecticut, one of the many short trips he was making, even during his years of solitude. He was able to accomplish this because his uncles were stagecoach owners.

1830:
Nathaniel Hawthorne published in the *Salem Gazette* his first story with the true "Hawthorne touch." It was called "The Hollow of the Three Hills."

1830–
1837:
Hawthorne began to publish regularly in various magazines and newspapers. He published for the first time, too, in *The Token,* an annual published by Samuel Griswold Goodrich.

1831:
In the summer of the year, Hawthorne traveled extensively by stagecoach in New Hampshire. He began to acquire ideas for such stories as "The Great Carbuncle."

Appendix

1832: Hawthorne traveled again in the fall of that year to New Hampshire and Vermont.

1833: Hawthorne each summer tried to get to some new spot near the sea. In the summer of 1833 he went to Swampscott. His observations of that village appear in a story called "The Village Uncle."

1836: For six months, Hawthorne edited a magazine entitled "The American Magazine of Useful and Entertaining Knowledge." It was a tedious job that required much hack writing. He and his sister Elizabeth, a very talented girl, did the work themselves.

1837: Nathaniel Hawthorne began to contribute to Samuel Goodrich's *Peter Parley Series for Children.* He wrote *Peter Parley's Universal History* with his sister Elizabeth. At the same time he was doing this almost tedious work, he brought out his first important work, *Twice-Told Tales.* Still unknown, the book had to be guaranteed financially by his friend, Horatio Bridge. That summer, from July 3rd to August 5th, Hawthorne visited Bridge in Augusta, Maine.

1838: In the summer and early fall, Hawthorne visited North Adams, Massachusetts, where some of the seeds of the great story, "Ethan Brand," were sown in his mind.

1838: Hawthorne became engaged to Sophia Peabody, one of the famous Peabody sisters of Salem.

1839–1840: Nathaniel Hawthorne became a weigher at the Custom House in Boston.

1841: Nathaniel Hawthorne published "Grandfather's Chair," a collection of historical stories of New England with a wide appeal to young readers.

1841: In April, Nathaniel Hawthorne moved to the Brook Farm community in West Roxbury, Massachusetts, where he hoped to be able to establish a home for Sophia. However, the experiment did not appeal to him and he left after eight months.

1842: Nathaniel Hawthorne married Sophia Peabody in the Peabody home in Boston on July 9th. It was one of the happiest of all marriages in the lives of literary men.

1842: A new edition of *Twice-Told Tales* was published in two volumes. In addition, Hawthorne published a book entitled *Biographical Stories.*

1842–
1845: Hawthorne lived at The Old Manse in Concord, when it was the heart of the American Renaissance in literature. Ralph Waldo Emerson, Henry David Thoreau, Margaret Fuller, Amos Bronson Alcott and his daughters—including the oldest, Louisa May—were just a few of his famous neighbors.

1842–
1845: Hawthorne wrote a variety of stories and tales which were published in the *Democratic Review.*

1844: Hawthorne's daughter Una was born. He named her for the character in the first book he had ever owned, Edward Spencer's *The Faerie Queene.*

1845: Hawthorne edited his friend Horatio Bridge's *Journal of an African Cruiser.*

1846: Hawthorne published his famous book, *Mosses from an Old Manse.*
On June 22nd of that year, his only son, Julian, was born.

1846–
1849: Hawthorne was a surveyor in the Salem Custom House. Although he appeared to have reached a dry point in his literary life, in effect his mind was storing up impressions that would emerge in his first great book, *The Scarlet Letter.* His mother died while he was writing his famous novel.

1850: *The Scarlet Letter* was published and immediately became a classic story of New England, America, and the world.

1850–
1851: The Hawthornes moved to the red house in Lenox, Massachusetts. A near neighbor was their good friend, Herman Melville, who would eventually publish *Moby Dick* and dedicate it to Nathaniel Hawthorne.

1851: On May 20th Hawthorne's second daughter and last child was born. This was a great year for the Hawthornes. Nathaniel published *The House of the Seven Gables, The Snow Image and Other Twice-Told Tales,* and *True Stories in History and Biography.*

1851–
1852: The Hawthornes moved to West Newton, Massachusetts, to the home of Hawthorne's brother-in-law, the great educator, Horace Mann.

1852: Once again Hawthorne published three books: *The Blithedale*

Romance, which had for its background his own experiences at Brook Farm; a very famous book for young people entitled *A Wonder Book for Girls and Boys;* and the controversial campaign biography of his friend, Franklin Pierce, who was campaigning for the presidency of the United States.

1852–
1853: The Hawthornes lived at The Wayside, in Concord, Massachusetts. Hawthorne called this house The Wayside because he felt he had once, as a young man, "sat down by the wayside of life like a man under enchantment."

1853: Hawthorne published his famous book for young people entitled *Tanglewood Tales for Girls and Boys.*

1853–
1857: Hawthorne was appointed United States Consul at Liverpool by his friend Franklin Pierce, who was now the President of the United States.

1857–
1859: The Hawthornes lived and traveled on the Continent. They lived in Rome and Florence. Hawthorne's notebooks for this period show a wide range of interests in art, Italy, and even the creative process. In *The Italian Notebooks* we can find the germ for his great novel, *The Marble Faun,* which is set in Italy.

1859: The Hawthornes returned to England, where Nathaniel finished the novel *The Marble Faun,* which had been begun in Florence in 1858. He needed the mist and cool of England, he said, to write his stories, just as he needed New England to be truly productive.

1860: *The Marble Faun* was published.
The Hawthornes returned to their home, The Wayside, in Concord. As the Civil War began to haunt New England, Hawthorne's health and happiness seemed to suffer. He tried desperately to write another romance, as he called his novels, but the results were only four unfinished fragments that were incomplete at his death. They were *Dr. Grimshawe's Secret, Septimius Felton, The Ancestral Footstep,* and *The Dolliver Romance.*

1862: During the spring, Hawthorne called on President Lincoln and wrote a famous piece called, "Chiefly About War Matters." He was a member of a delegation from Massachusetts.

1863: Hawthorne published, and dedicated to his friend Franklin Pierce, a book entitled *Our Old Home,* essays on England, the

English, and English-American relations that interested him
strongly. There are many insights on both countries in this
very rewarding book.

1864: On May 19th, at Plymouth, New Hampshire, Nathaniel
Hawthorne died. He was buried on May 23rd at Sleepy Hollow Cemetery in Concord.

Selected Books by and About
Nathaniel Hawthorne

As of this writing, the definitive bibliography of Hawthorne's work has yet to appear. It will be titled *Nathaniel Hawthorne: An Annotated Biography*, by Nouvart Tashjian and Dwight Eckerman. It will eventually be a book of more than four hundred pages. At the present time, however, the available bibliographies are three: Nina E. Browne's *A Bibliography of Nathaniel Hawthorne*, W. H. Cathcart's *Bibliography of the Works of Nathaniel Hawthorne*, and J. C. Chamberlain's *First Editions of Nathaniel Hawthorne*. All of these bibliographies, however, appeared in the very early twentieth century. The major assessment of Hawthorne and some of the best of all critical work appeared closer to our own times.

The famous edition of Hawthorne's own work, The Riverside Edition, is *The Complete Works of Nathaniel Hawthorne*, edited by G. P. Lathrop, published by Houghton Mifflin in 1883 in twelve volumes. Other editions also are available. The complete *Writings* or so called *Autographed Edition*, Boston, 1900; and *The Old Manse Edi-*

tion, Boston, 1900. *The American Notebooks of Nathaniel Hawthorne*, edited by Randall Stewart in 1932, and *The English Notebooks of Nathaniel Hawthorne*, edited by Randall Stewart in 1941, are both invaluable. Professor Norman Holmes Pearson is now working on *The Italian Notebooks*.

Young and old book collectors will find a variety of titles by Nathaniel Hawthorne in many bookshops, particularly those in New England, where he was and is a household word.

A new anthology of his stories, excerpts from his letters, notebooks, vignettes of his friends and places to which he made "literary pilgrimages," especially selected for young people, with particular emphasis on Hawthorne's own creative process and the background of the stories, has been selected by me and is to be issued simultaneously with this biography under the title *A Hawthorne Treasury*.

It is always exciting for young researchers to gather their material from a variety of contemporary sources, and Hawthorne is a particularly attractive subject when handled in this way. His name appears in nearly all the books by the famous authors of the American Renaissance. You will find him discussed by his wife, by his son, by his daughter, by his son-in-law G. P. Lathrop, by his friends Horatio Bridge and Ralph Waldo Emerson, as well as by his publisher and other friends. The manuscripts of most interest are scattered throughout the United States. They are in the Boston Public Library, The Essex Institute (Salem, the Manning Collection), the Henry Huntington Library, the Houghton Library at Harvard, the National Archives in Washington, D. C., the Duyckinck and Berg Collection of the New York Public Library, and the Pierpont Morgan Library.

A new edition of Hawthorne's magnificent letters is being prepared by Professor Norman Holmes Pearson and Professor Randall Stewart. Until such a book is available there will continue to be inconsistencies in the publication of Hawthorne's letters, printed as they have been from a variety of sources. Hawthorne scholars have made a great effort to restore texts in both letters and notebooks that were tampered with in the nineteenth century.

Here is a selected list of books that were helpful in preparing this book:

Andrews, Charles M., *The Colonial Period of American History*, Vols. I, II, III, IV. New Haven: Yale University Press, 1938.
Arvin, Newton, *Hawthorne*. New York: Russell & Russell, 1961.
Atkinson, Brooks, *Walden and Other Writings of Henry David Thoreau*. New York: Random House, Inc., 1937.

Austin, George Lowell, *Henry Wadsworth Longfellow: His Life, His Works, His Friendships.* Boston: Lee and Shepard, 1883.

Bartlett, George B., *Concord (Historic, Literary and Picturesque).* Boston: Lothrop Publishing Co., 1885.

Bennett, James O'Donnell, *Much Loved Books.* New York: Liveright Publishing Co., 1927.

Bewley, Marius, *The Complex Fate: Hawthorne, Henry James and Some Other American Writers.* London: Chatto & Windus, 1952.

Blair, Walter, "Nathaniel Hawthorne," *Eight American Authors: A Review of Research and Criticism,* ed. Floyd Stovall. New York: Modern Language Association of America, 1956.

Bode, Carl, *The American Lyceum (Town Meeting of the Mind).* New York: Oxford University Press, 1956.

Brooks, Van Wyck, *The Flowering of New England.* New York: E. P. Dutton & Co., Inc., 1936.

Brooks, Van Wyck, *New England's Indian Summer.* New York: E. P. Dutton & Co., Inc., 1940.

Brooks, Van Wyck, *The Times of Melville and Whitman.* New York: E. P. Dutton & Co., Inc., 1947.

Brown, Arthur W., *Margaret Fuller.* New York: Twayne Publishers, Inc., 1964.

Burlingame, Robert, *The American Conscience.* New York: Alfred A. Knopf, 1957.

Cantwell, Robert, *Nathaniel Hawthorne: The American Years.* New York: Rinehart & Company, Inc., 1948.

Chapman, Maria Weston, *Harriet Martineau's Autobiography.* Boston: Houghton, Mifflin & Co., 1885.

Charvat, William, *Literary Publishing in America,* 1790–1850. Philadelphia: University of Pennsylvania Press, 1959.

Cheney, Ednah D., *Louisa May Alcott: Her Life, Letters, and Journals.* Boston: Roberts Brothers, 1890.

Chipperfield, Faith, *In Quest of Love.* New York: Coward-McCann, Inc., 1957.

Commager, Henry Steele, *Theodore Parker: An Anthology.* Boston: Beacon Press, 1960.

The Complete Works of Nathaniel Hawthorne, Riverside Edition, 12 vols. Boston: Houghton Mifflin Company, 1883.

The Complete Writings of Nathaniel Hawthorne, Old Manse Edition, 22 vols. Boston: Houghton Mifflin Company, 1900.

Cook, Clarence, *A Girl's Life Eighty Years Ago: Selections from the Letters of Eliza Southgate Bowne.* New York: Charles Scribner's Sons, 1887.

Curtis, Edith Roelker, *A Season in Utopia: The Story of Brook Farm.* New York: Thomas Nelson & Sons, 1961.

Davidson, Edward H., *Hawthorne's Last Phase.* New Haven: Yale University Press, 1949.

Donohue, Agnes McNeill, *The Hawthorne Question.* New York: Thomas Y. Crowell Co., 1963.

Drake, Samuel Adams, *Old Landmarks and Historic Fields of Middlesex.* Boston: Roberts Brothers, 1888.

Dupee, F. W., *Henry James.* New York: Dell Publishing Co., A Delta Book, 1965.

Early, Eleanor, *A New England Sampler.* Boston: Waverly House, 1946.

Edwards, Agnes, *The Romantic Shore.* Salem: Salem Press Co., 1915.

Emerson, Ralph Waldo, *Letters and Social Aims.* Boston: Houghton, Mifflin & Co., 1884.

Emerson, Ralph Waldo, *Collected Works of Ralph Waldo Emerson.* New York: Greystone Press, 1956.

Emerson, Ralph Waldo, *Natural History of Intellect and Other Papers.* New York: Sully and Kleinteich, 1893.

Emerson, Ralph Waldo, *Lectures and Biographical Sketches.* New York: Sully and Kleinteich, 1893.

Essex Institute, The, *Essex Institute Historical Collections: Special Hawthorne Issue,* Vol. C., No. 4. Salem: The Essex Institute, 1964.

Essex Institute, The, *Visitor's Guide to Salem.* Salem: The Essex Institute, 1937.

Fick, Leonard J., *The Light Beyond: A Study of Hawthorne's Theology.* Westminster, Md.: The Newman Press, 1955.

Fiedler, Leslie, *Love and Death in the American Novel.* New York: Criterion Books, 1960.

Fields, James T., *Yesterdays with Authors.* Boston: Houghton, Mifflin & Co., 1899.

Fogle, Richard H., *Hawthorne's Fiction: The Light and the Dark.* Norman, Okla.: University of Oklahoma Press, 1952.

Foster, Charles H., *Beyond Concord: Selected Writings of David Atwood Wasson.* Bloomington: Indiana University Press, 1965.

Froebels, Friedrich, *Pedagogies of the Kindergarten.* New York: D. Appleton & Co., 1906.

Gilder, J. L., and J. B., *Authors at Home.* New York: Cassell & Co., Ltd., 1888.

Gohdes, Clarence, *American Literature in Nineteenth Century England*. Carbondale, Ill.: Southern Illinois University Press, 1944.

Goodspeed, Charles, *Nathaniel Hawthorne and the Museum of the Salem East India Marine Society*. Salem: Peabody Museum, 1946.

Gorman, Herbert, *Hawthorne: A Study in Solitude*. New York: George H. Doran Company, 1927.

Greenslet, Ferris, *The Lowells and Their Seven Worlds*. Boston: Houghton Mifflin Company, 1946.

Hale, Nancy, *New England Discovery*. New York: Coward-McCann, Inc., 1963.

Hanscom, Elizabeth Deering, *The Friendly Craft: A Collection of American Letters*. New York: The Macmillan Company, 1909.

Hanscom, Elizabeth Deering, *Hawthorne and His Circle*. New York: Harper & Brothers, 1903.

Hanscom, Elizabeth Deering, *Hawthorne Reading*. Cleveland: Rowfant Club, 1902.

Hawthorne, Hildegarde, *Romantic Rebel: The Story of Nathaniel Hawthorne*. New York: Appleton-Century-Crofts, 1932.

Nathaniel Hawthorne: The American Notebooks, ed. Randall Stewart. New Haven: Yale University Press, 1932.

Hawthorne, Julian, *Nathaniel Hawthorne and His Wife*. Boston: Houghton, Mifflin & Co., 1896.

Hawthorne, Nathaniel, *The House of the Seven Gables*. Columbus: Ohio State University Press, 1965.

Hawthorne, Nathaniel, *The Blithedale Romance and Fanshawe*. Columbus: Ohio State University Press, 1964.

Hawthorne, Nathaniel, *The Scarlet Letter*. Columbus: Ohio State University Press, 1962.

Hawthorne, Nathaniel, *Twice-Told Tales and Other Short Stories*. New York: Washington Square Press, Inc., 1960.

Hawthorne, Nathaniel, *The Complete Novels and Selected Tales*. New York: The Modern Library of Random House, Inc., 1937.

Hawthorne, Nathaniel, *Moses from an Old Manse*. Boston: Houghton, Mifflin & Co., 1882.

Hawthorne, Nathaniel, *Passages from the French and Italian Notebooks of Nathaniel Hawthorne*. Boston: Houghton, Mifflin & Co., 1871.

Hawthorne, Nathaniel, *Passages from the English Notebooks of Nathaniel Hawthorne*. Boston: Houghton, Mifflin & Co., 1870.

Hawthorne, Nathaniel, *Passages from the American Notebooks of Nathaniel Hawthorne*. Boston: Houghton, Mifflin & Co., 1868.

Hawthorne, Nathaniel, *The Snow-Image and Other Twice-Told*

Tales by Nathaniel Hawthorne. Boston: Houghton, Mifflin & Co., 1851.

Hawthorne, Nathaniel, *True Stories from History and Biography by Nathaniel Hawthorne.* Boston: Houghton, Mifflin & Co., 1850.

Haywood, Charles F., *Minutemen and Marines.* New York: Dodd, Mead & Co., 1963.

Henderson, Helen W., *A Loiterer in New England.* New York: George H. Doran Co., 1919.

Hoeltje, Hubert H., *Inward Sky: The Mind and Heart of Nathaniel Hawthorne.* Durham, N.C.: Duke University Press, 1962.

Holmes, Oliver Wendell, *The Autocrat of the Breakfast Table.* New York: New American Library, 1961.

Holmes, Oliver Wendell, *Pages from an Old Volume of Life.* Boston: Houghton, Mifflin & Co., 1883.

Hutton, Laurence, *Literary Landmarks of Florence.* New York: Harper & Brothers Publishers, 1897.

Hutton, Richard Holt, *Essays in Literary Criticism.* Philadelphia: Jos. H. Coates & Co., 1876.

James, Henry, *Autobiography.* New York: Criterion Books, Inc., 1956.

James, Henry, *Hawthorne.* ("English Men of Letters Series.") London: The Macmillan Company, 1879.

Johnson, Clifton, *Old-Time Schools and School-Books.* New York: The Macmillan Company, 1904.

Kane, A. N., *Hawthorne: A Collection of Critical Essays.* Englewood Cliffs, N.J.: Prentice-Hall, Inc., 1966.

Larcom, Lucy, *A New England Girlhood.* New York: Corinth Books, 1961.

Lathrop, George Parsons, *A Study of Hawthorne.* Boston: J. R. Osgood, 1876.

Lathrop, Rose Hawthorne, *Memories of Hawthorne.* Boston: Houghton, Mifflin Company, 1897.

Levin, David, *What Happened in Salem?* New York: Harcourt, Brace & World, Inc., 1960.

Levin, Harry, *The Power of Blackness: Hawthorne, Poe, Melville.* New York: Alfred A. Knopf, Inc., 1958.

Leyda, Jay, *The Melville Log,* 2 vols. New York: Harcourt, Brace & Co., 1951.

Longfellow, Henry Wadsworth, *Favorite Poems of Henry Wadsworth Longfellow,* ed. Henry Seidel Canby. Garden City, N.Y.: Doubleday & Co., Inc., 1947.

Male, Roy R., *Hawthorne's Tragic Vision.* New York: Norton Library Edition, W. W. Norton & Co., Inc., 1964.

Martin, Terence, *Nathaniel Hawthorne*. New York: Twayne Publishers, Inc., 1965.

Mather, Edward, *Nathaniel Hawthorne*. New York: Thomas Y. Crowell Co., 1940.

Matthiessen, F. O., *American Renaissance*. New York: Oxford University Press, 1941.

Messer, N. S., *Streets and Homes in Old Salem*. Prepared and Published by N. S. Messer, August 1919–1959; Revised 1960 and 1963 by E. C. Early.

Miller, Perry, *Margaret Fuller: American Romantic*. Garden City, N.Y.: Anchor Books, Doubleday & Co., Inc., 1963.

Miller, Perry, *Errand into the Wilderness*. Cambridge, Mass.: The Belknap Press of Harvard University Press, 1956.

Morison, Samuel Eliot, *The Intellectual Life of Colonial New England*. Ithaca, N.Y.: Cornell University Press, 1965.

Morison, Samuel Eliot, *Builders of the Bay Colony*. Boston: Sentry Edition, Houghton Mifflin Company, 1964.

Paul, Sherman, *Thoreau: A Collection of Critical Essays*. Englewood Cliffs, N.J.: Prentice-Hall, Inc., 1962.

Peattie, Roderick, *The Berkshires*. New York: The Vanguard Press, Inc., 1948.

Perry, Bliss, *The Heart of Emerson's Journals*. New York: Dover Edition, Dover Publications, Inc., 1958.

Phillips, Mary E., *Reminiscences of William Wetmore Story*. Chicago: Rand, McNally & Co., 1897.

Sams, Henry W., *Autobiography of Brook Farm*. Engelwood Cliffs, N.J.: Prentice-Hall, Inc., 1958.

Schubert, Leland, *Hawthorne, The Artist: Fine-Art Devices in Fiction*. Chapel Hill, N.C.: University of North Carolina Press, 1944.

Scudder, Townsend, *Concord: American Town*. Boston: Little, Brown & Co., 1947.

Shackleton, Robert, *The Book of Boston*. Philadelphia: The Penn Publishing Co., 1930.

Silliman, Augustus E., *A Gallop Among American Scenery*. New York: A. S. Barnes & Co., 1881.

Silsbee, M. C. D., *A Half Century in Salem*. Boston: Houghton, Mifflin & Co., 1887.

Stapleton, Laurence, *A Writer's Journal* (*H. D. Thoreau*). London: Heinemann, 1961.

Starkey, Marion L., *The Devil in Massachusetts*. New York: Alfred A. Knopf, Inc., 1949.

Appendix

Stein, William B., *Hawthorne's Faust: A Study of the Devil Archetype*. Gainesville, Fla.: University of Florida Press, 1953.

Stewart, Randall, *Nathaniel Hawthorne: A Biography*. New Haven: Yale University Press, 1948.

Stoddard, R. H., *et al.*, *Poets' Homes*. Boston: D. Lothrop & Co., 1877.

Stovall, Floyd, *Eight American Authors*. New York: W. W. Norton & Co., Inc., 1963.

Strout, Cushing, *Hawthorne in England*. Ithaca, N.Y.: Cornell University Press, 1965.

Swift, Lindsay, *Brook Farm*. New York: Corinth Books, Inc., 1900.

Tharp, Louise Hall, *The Peabody Sisters of Salem*. Boston: Little, Brown & Co., 1950.

Thaxter, Rosamond, *Sandpiper (The Life & Letters of Celia Thaxter)*. Francistown: Marshall Jones Co., 1963.

Thoreau, Henry David, *The River: Selections from the Journal*. New York: Twayne Publishers, Inc., 1963.

Thoreau, Henry David, *Walden and Selected Essays*. Chicago: Packard & Co., 1947.

Thoreau, Henry David, *A Week on the Concord and Merrimac Rivers*. London: J. M. Dent & Sons, Ltd., 1849.

Thurston, Jarvis, *et al.*, *Short Fiction Criticism: A Checklist of Interpretation Since 1925 of Stories and Novelettes 1800–1958*. Denver: Alan Swallow, 1960.

Thwing, Annie Haven, *The Crooked and Narrow Streets of the Town of Boston, 1630–1822*. Boston: Marshall Jones Co., 1920.

Ticknor, Caroline, *Dr. Holmes's Boston*. Boston: Houghton Mifflin Company, 1915.

Trask, Georgianne and Burkhart, Charles, *Storytellers and Their Art*. Garden City, N.Y.: Doubleday & Co., Inc., 1963.

Trowbridge, J. T. and Larcom, Lucy, *Our Young Folks Magazine*. Boston: James R. Osgood & Co., 1872.

Tryon, W. S., *Parnassus Corner: A Life of James T. Fields*. Boston: Houghton Mifflin Company, 1963.

Turner, Arlin, *Nathaniel Hawthorne*. New York: Barnes & Noble, Inc., 1961.

Underwood, Francis H., *Henry Wadsworth Longfellow*. Boston: James R. Osgood & Co., 1882.

Van Doren, Mark, *Nathaniel Hawthorne*. New York: The Viking Press, 1957.

Vaughan, Alden T., *New England Frontier: Puritans and Indians 1620–1675*. Boston: Little, Brown & Co., 1965.

Wagenknecht, Edward, *Longfellow: A Full-Length Portrait*. New York: Longmans, Green & Co., 1955.

Wagenknecht, Edward, *Nathaniel Hawthorne: Man and Writer.* New York: Oxford University Press, 1961.

Waggoner, Hyatt H., *Hawthorne.* Cambridge, Mass.: The Belknap Press of Harvard University Press, 1963.

Whipple, Edwin Percy, *Recollections of Eminent Men.* Boston: Ticknor & Co., 1886.

Williams, Oscar and Honig, Edwin, *The Mentor Book of Major American Poets.* New York: New American Library, 1962.

Wilson, Edmund, *The Shock of Recognition.* New York: Doubleday, Doran & Co., Inc., 1943.

Wilson, Rufus Rockwell, *New England in Letters.* New York: A. Wessels Co., 1904.

Wolfe, Theodore F., *A Literary Pilgrimage.* Philadelphia: J. B. Lippincott Co., 1895.

Wolfe, Theodore F., *Literary Shrines.* Philadelphia: J. B. Lippincott Co., 1895.

✏ *Acknowledgments* ✏

Every book has its inception far back in time and space, but I do remember within the last decade a glorious Massachusetts spring day in a garden by the sea—the sort of landscape that most attracted Hawthorne—when I first undertook serious thought about this book. Nathaniel Hawthorne had long been a commanding figure to me, not only during my school days, many of which were spent around his own Massachusetts haunts of Concord, Salem, and Boston, but also because of my pervasive interest in the literary groups of our country. Though Hawthorne was a peripheral member of the Concord Group, he absorbed and used the ferment of his times.

That Massachusetts garden belonged to my friends Robert and Marguerite Sheffield, whose library of New England authors is extraordinary.

Both their daughters, Ann and Sally Sheffield, have often been an inspiration to me, and were particularly so in this book. My nephews, too, Charles and Richard Manley, have been close to this project, and my nieces, Sara and Carol Lewis, have helped in the actual preparation of it. Sara gave me great assistance with the bibliography, and Carol, as did my daughter Shivaun, took several interesting Concord photographs.

I would especially like to thank Miss Marilyn Nicoson of Concord, who has both made a special study of Hawthorne's writing and taught it in his own town; she has an enviable intimacy with his life and an extraordinary grasp of his work and his meaning to American culture. Mr. David Proper of the Essex Institute was also of invaluable assistance, but any interpretation of Hawthorne and his times are my own and do not reflect those of the Institute, to which I am also indebted for both information and photographs. Professor Norman Holmes Pearson offered help, and I have drawn heavily upon his published sources. I am thankful, too, to Mrs. William Moss of the Concord Free Library, and to the Peabody Museum of Salem, not only for its assistance in acquiring photographs but for the many hours of pleasure the museum has given me in the past and for its still remarkable ability to evoke the days of Hawthorne and of Salem's great glory.

I am grateful to Mr. Charles Krentzman of Brookline, Massachusetts; Mr. Ted Valpey of Holliston; Mrs. Emily Gibson, formerly of Lee, Massachusetts, who was most helpful with her background knowledge of Hawthorne in the Berkshires. My sister Gogo Lewis, who has been involved with so many of my books, as I have been involved with hers, was also of great assistance.

Susan L. Belcher has been, as she always will be, of enormous help. My husband Robert Manley shared my life with Nathaniel Hawthorne for the years it took me to brood about and finally write this book, and he helped, as well, to locate important current references. I wish to thank, too, the Bowdoin College Library, the Berkshire Athenaeum, and Mr. Edward Naumburg, whose knowledge of the location of Hawthorne manuscripts and memorabilia was invaluable to me.

Acknowledgments

I have been fortunate to have Mrs. Grace Schiro assist with the preparation of this manuscript, and I deeply appreciate the care given it by Mrs. Mary McCabe.

Miscellaneous material, documents, and books have come to me from a variety of sources. Mrs. Teddy Bookman and Mrs. Evelyn Erb of the Country Bumpkin in Locust Valley located some interesting material. Philip Hurbert of the Sou'wester Bookshop in Bellport, New York, supplied me with new titles about Hawthorne, and, above all, Mason Foley of the Hingham Bookshop in Hingham, Massachusetts, kept me fully informed of all his acquisitions covering the New England Renaissance. The Pangloss Bookshop in Cambridge, Massachusetts, has been, for this book as it has been for others, a most useful source, as has been Marc Thompson of the Thompson Book Store in Sea Cliff, New York.

Mrs. Jane Brown, Mrs. Mab Gray, Mr. and Mrs. Frank Manley, and Mr. Peter Kotsogean all supplied some source of inspiration between the time of inception and the finished book.

As always, I am grateful to the Vanguard Press for its care in preparing the manuscript for the printer. Mrs. Bernice Woll and Miss Muriel Fuller were particularly helpful, and I have relied on Mr. Ralph Paterline in my choice of illustrations.